D1631200

HOW TO ROB BANKS WITHOUT VIOLENCE

HOW TO ROB BANKS WITHOUT VIOLENCE / Roderic Knowles

PHASE FOUR.

THE UNTAMED

TOULON FIX

RENEGADE

THE VIPERS

SNAKES WITH GUNS

STUNGUNS

MICHAEL JOSEPH LONDON

First published in Great Britain by
Michael Joseph Limited
52 Bedford Square
London WC1
MAY 1972
SECOND IMPRESSION JULY 1972

7181 1003 X

Printed in Great Britain by
Hollen Street Press Ltd, at Slough
and bound by
James Burn at Esher, Surrey.

Preface

This book was written in a Dutch prison, in a code which took as long again to decipher. It describes, with no embellishment, two large-scale international criminal operations organised by the author.

The question may be asked, why did someone of his background – born into a rich aristocratic family, educated at Eton, and after a life seriously engaged in various literary, artistic and philosophical pursuits – become a criminal?

An autobiographical note, while not necessary for an appreciation of the plot, appears as Appendix B, and may be of interest to some readers.

Contents

The endpapers show the standard instructions for making the Smuggler's Suit, and a 'Carrier' putting the suit on.

PART ONE

Chapter 1/A Conversation

'Shoot, man, shoot,' yelled Sebastian defiantly.

He stood dimly outlined against the wall at the far end of the large basement patio. This, grandly referred to as the archery range, was one of several luxuries of the hundred-guinea a week Belgravia flat rented by the Honourable Mr Featherington-Smythe and myself for the running of our poker games. It was five in the morning and still dark. I stood by the open window of the ground-floor drawing room with a bow in my hands and an arrow held lightly in firing position. Behind me one of our bi-weekly games was in progress. Ben, one of three croupiers, immaculate in evening dress, was dealing a round of five card stud with his usual inexhaustible verve. Grouped round the green baize cloth in eager anticipation, although looking the worse for wear after eight intensive hours of play, were the punters: a young merchant banker; a member of Lloyds, son of one of Britain's largest race-horse owners; an out-of-work and near-impoverished expatriate Polish count; Lord Wareham, a rake and lunatic gambler; and a young advertising executive.

'King to bet,' snapped Ben, who had not heard Sebastian's shouts, due to excessive chatter around the room. 'Bring us another coffee, luv,' he called to one of the girls. These games were lavish affairs. We provided pleasant surroundings, employed the croupiers as well as a secretary and doorman, guaranteed the credit, made freely available the best in food and drink and had them served along with any small needs of punters by the most scintillating and elegant young females that could be found – mostly models or ex-debs. The function of the doorman was to warn against the advent of the law and keep non-participants out.

'Less noise in the background, please,' demanded Ben, addressing himself particularly to a party of three who had just arrived from the Clermont Club, then glancing at me who did not look at that moment, with bow in hand, conducive to any quiet atmosphere. Profit, ten per cent on each winning pot, depended on the frequency of rounds dealt. Ben's great contribution to the games was not only his amazing repertoire of chat which created an ambiance in which punters could enjoy losing their money, if that was at all possible, but also his ability to keep the game at a rapid pace, by his skill in dealing and by eliminating distractions.

'One more queen and it would have been a full house,' murmured Lord Wareham.

'What about the nines?'

'They were dead.'

'I'm off,' said one of the punters. He had no chips to cash in. The game was coming to an end.

'Go on. Shoot man,' yelled Sebastian again.

I took aim.

He didn't move.

'Get away from the target or you'll be sorry. I'll give you five seconds to move, then I'm going to shoot. One . . . Two . . . Three . . . '

'Come on man, you've got no bum, that's your trouble. Shoot!'

'Four . . . '

The bow was still pointing at him as I bent it back to its full width.

'Five . . . '

'Come on. Shoot!'

I slackened the pressure of the bow which was likely to launch an arrow whether I wanted it to or not.

'Move, Sebastian, or I'm going to shoot . . . NOW.' I aimed between his legs and stretched the bow to its full capacity – No change of mind? – None – I fired.

'Christ man!' he screamed. 'Christ, you've got me. It's all over. You've got me.'

The light was too bad to see what I had got, but he was hopping all over the place.

'You could have killed me, man. Christ man, you could have ruined me. Pinned my valuables to the walls. Right through my trousers! Would you believe it! Right through my trousers. You've grazed my leg.'

Apart from a small scratch and bruise Sebastian was really none the worse for his adventure. In fact it was obvious that he was pleased about it. He left the archery range and wandered back into the drawing-room smiling, grabbed an audience, and explained to them for the first of a hundred times what had happened.

Although the party broke up shortly afterwards, as things turned out, the day had just significantly begun.

'I never thought it possible he'd have an ace in the hole. There were three showing, and after that previous bluff . . . ' Featherington-Smythe droned on, and Sebastian demonstrated his boredom by going off to bed. Tania, my girl-friend, had done so earlier.

'Knowles,' said Ben, 'Now you've done the books, shot Sebastian, and gambled away all the profits – what about a Scotch?'

We sat down and began to talk.

Ben came from the west country, from a working-class family. At fourteen he had run away to sea. Later, he had become a part-time actor and stuntman, and an excellent amateur golfer. For several years he had been part of the London gambling scene, as assistant to the well-known London club-owner, Raymond Nash – who in his turn had been henchman to the notorious property villain, Peter Rachmann.

Ben talked of Raymond; and I was interested as I had known Raymond myself even earlier than Ben. What I did not know was that he had subsequently gone into gold smuggling and that others I knew had gone in with him. Raymond had been in the business three years, made a lot of money, but finally came unstuck in Tokyo through sheer stupidity. Ben himself had been closely involved in Raymond's activities. He had begun as a carrier, then become one of his representatives in the Far East, and finally his right-hand man. The figures being mentioned were in hundreds of thousands of pounds, so the subject, about which I knew absolutely nothing, began to interest me a great deal. Why, I thought, could I or we not do the same thing? Might not Ben possess sufficient know-how and contacts to make a start? Making no effort to hide my interest I examined him on his experiences in exhaustive detail. Featherington-Smythe was having similar thoughts and listened eagerly.

'How much did you get paid as a carrier?' I asked.

'About a hundred and fifty quid. It varied. I was also on a percentage.'

'Why was Raymond caught in Tokyo with five carriers' loads in his hotel room? Why hadn't he sold it? Couldn't he?'

'Of course he could. He had customers lined up waiting for it. He was a megalomaniac. He was much more involved with his fantasies and image than with making money. He just liked to hoard it. He liked to see it piling up, to sit round it, dance round it, hold parties round it, showing everyone what a big shot he was. Gold, diamonds, pearls, the lot. He should never have been there in the first place.'

'What happened to him?'

'He was lucky. He got off with a suspended sentence of eighteen months.'

'Why didn't you go back into business with him afterwards?'

'He started mucking me around. We had a big fight over twenty quid. Why should I do him up for twenty quid when I had personally saved him twenty grand?'

'Why didn't you go back into the business yourself?

'I thought about it, but I haven't been able to raise the capital.'

'How much would you need?'

'Twenty grand, about.'

'Surely there must be loads of people around who would jump at the idea?'

'If there are, I haven't been able to find them.'

I found this very difficult to believe, but, on reflection, realised that Ben was no organiser. I had heard him described as 'The most incredible personality I have ever come across', but he was no organiser. He talked in vague wild fantastic terms with little regard for concrete fact or figures and was unable to present any reasonable proposition.

'Well, I'll raise it,' I said finally – hopefully.

'I'll raise it,' insisted Featherington-Smythe.

We left this point unargued. Ben left for his own flat and Featherington-Smythe went off to his ten foot by seven foot bed.

My mind was already made up. This was the break I had been waiting for. I was determined that Ben and I would go into business. I would learn everything there was to learn about gold. When I had done this I would work out our plans and procedures as if we were actually ready to start, and also a proposition that would convince even the most hard-headed businessman. I didn't fear Featherington-Smythe, believing that he would never in a million years come to any point of action. We had one thing in common: we were both stony broke.

Shortly after this our private poker games packed up. We had blown our profits, exhausted our supply of punters and the off-season had approached. Apart from the fact that I had come across Ben and found a proposition that was workable, if only I could raise the capital for it, I was back to square one. But it was important not to appear broke. Ben was under the impression that I had some capital to contribute and that we would not really have to raise much extra. Since this was so far from the truth, it was necessary to avoid him until I had even a small amount. He was going to have to be conned into committing himself to preparing and setting up an organisation from a position of virtual impecunity, otherwise he would dismiss our chances of making a start as utterly remote. So I put it about that I would be going abroad for most of the summer and waited hopefully for an expected thousand pounds from a grandfather's trust.

After a long desperate summer, it came. I recontacted Ben, whose predicament had been even worse than mine. We were both anxious to get our teeth into something and decided to get straight to work.

Chapter 2/The Theory

Ben was thirty-five and about five-foot-nine, always tanned, and looked athletic and tough. His face was well-worn, with strong laughter lines around mischievously twinkly and inquisitive dark blue eyes. He had a tremendous capacity for living, and was the creator of life around him. He never felt out of place anywhere or with anyone, he had so much personality. This personality got under everyone's guard. He was crude, called a spade a spade, and had no pretentions about anything. He had such a strong sense of fun that it was impossible not to like him. To women he was irresistible. He had always lived from day to day, one moment having lots of money, the next moment none. How he got it really didn't matter. He could no more save than fly to the moon. It was obvious that he had no business brain, that he was a playboy at heart, and that any idea of prolonged work would be anathema to him.

As for me, he had loathed me from the first few minutes. I was his boss. I stood for everything he hated. I gave orders, put work before play, imposed disciplines. But strangely this hatred turned to respect – perhaps helped by a realisation that I had what he needed for this business, just as in other respects, for his experience, his superb qualities as a salesman, and confidence-winner, I needed him.

We agreed to form a partnership. Ben suggested that I took seventy-five per cent of the profits, which he reckoned to be reasonable as I would be raising all the capital. I argued that the most satisfactory relationship would develop if we both had the same interest. We agreed on the latter.

I decided to trust him absolutely which, in view of the fact that our entire finances would frequently be at his disposal, was a major decision. I had good reasons. First, though he was a rogue, I believed he was a man of great personal integrity. Secondly, if one could not place this trust in a partner it was better to have no partnership at all. Thirdly, I could not envisage a time when we would not be indispensable to each other. I had also confirmed that Ben had indeed demonstrated great personal loyalty to Raymond at the time of his downfall in Tokyo. At the time of his arrest, Ben had had £20,000 belonging to Raymond. He had taken the first plane out to Hong Kong, placed this money in Raymond's account, and caught the next plane back to Tokyo to engage a lawyer.

The vital question now was whether *Ben* could re-establish his contacts and find anyone willing to resume business. Raymond's downfall had been much publicised and Ben didn't know whether any of the customers had been embarrassed or affected by this. Even if they had not, it would still be understandable if none showed any willingness to have anything further to do with anyone connected with the same set-up. Most *customers*, Ben told me, were businessmen with important positions, who had a lot more to lose than those who smuggled. Usually they were not allowed to own gold and certainly not imported gold with foreign markings. Many bought it in order to evade taxes. Neither they, nor the agents who made their lives out of these transactions, would risk exposure and ruin by dealing with people they didn't believe to be wholly reliable. For this reason it was impossible for *outsiders* to break into the market in any country without at least one strong connection; and as we couldn't afford to send Ben out to the Far East on a reconnaissance trip we decided that we had to have a letter from at least one customer, confirming his willingness to co-operate. Without this we might be wasting our time.

Anticipating a favourable reply to our letter, we continued our preparations. We had decided to do our buying in Europe – in Brussels or Geneva, where it was legal to do so – and run our first loads into Hong Kong which was the easiest country to enter and where Ben's contacts were the strongest.

The first thing I had to do was to familiarise myself with everything Ben knew about the business. The second way of getting at information was to carry out my own research. In this I had an assistant. Adam.

I had met Adam nine months earlier and he had become the doorman at our games. Prior to this, despite his public schooling and having studied – briefly – at the Bar, he had been selling fluffy animals in Oxford Street. He was quiet, unobtrusive, ineffective, and lazy, but he was loyal and discreet. Ben had insisted that because of his excellent appearance, always well and elegantly dressed despite his means, he would be a good carrier. It seemed to me that he could be trained to administrate.

On the basis of my research I made endless calculations. I discovered that the official price of gold in Hong Kong was quoted in Hong Kong dollars per tael. This I converted into US dollars per troy ounce (with one tael equalling 1.215 ounces), then US dollars per kilo, then Belgian francs and pounds sterling per kilo. In order to save time in the future I produced instant conversion tables. We collected information not only on Hong Kong but Tokyo, Manila, Bangkok, Singapore, South Korea, Indonesia and Taiwan. We had decided to leave out India even though it was reputed to be one of the world's largest black markets, worth in the region of two hundred million dollars a year. Two of Raymond's boys had been stopped there, besides which we both felt uneasy about the idea of doing business with Indians. According to one source, a well-known international economist, the price there was 100 dollars an ounce. More reliable sources, including Ben, put it at around seventy dollars – still double the fixed international price but not in our opinion worth certain aggravation and loss.

I obtained details of currencies, weights, costs of fares,

times and routes of flights and the frequencies of arrivals and departures, train schedules, particulars of visa and vaccination requirements on entry, permitted lengths of stay and so forth. Maps were bought and English language papers that were likely to quote gold and currency rates as well as news on any exposed smuggling operations. Cuttings were extracted and filed.

At that time the international buying price of gold was controlled. It had been fixed by President Roosevelt in 1934 at around thirty-five dollars an ounce. All I needed to do was to add to the cost of a return fare two hundred pounds to cover the carrier's fee and the same for overheads, and I would have a good idea of the possible profits per trip. This amounted to a couple of thousand pounds. Our goal however was not to make occasional large sums as Raymond had done by sending in carriers every now and again, but to work out a system which would yield regular payments amounting to millions of pounds a year.

Playing about with figures I could see that the original minimum figure Ben had quoted – £20,000 – was an exaggeration. We had agreed to limit our load to twenty-four kilos, which required a capital investment of £11,500. I discovered, however, that it was possible to start with a great deal less; £5,750 would buy a load of twelve kilos, the proceeds from which could be transferred back by cable to Brussels. The profit could then be invested in a bigger load and so on, until the maximum load had been reached.

The first problem was to find out how many times a week one unit of capital could be turned over. The greater the frequency, the less the burden of fixed overhead costs and the sooner we would reach our maximum load. The answer depended on the speed with which the proceeds of a sale could be transferred from the Far East back to Europe for re-purchasing. In our favour was the eight hour difference between Hong Kong and Central European time. This meant that it was theoretically possible to go into a bank in Hong Kong at nine o'clock in the morning on a Wednesday (for example) with thirty thousand dollars in cash, with instructions for the sum to be transferred urgently by telex. A few minutes later in our bank in Brussels details of the transfer would appear on the receiving telex machine at one o'clock the same morning – that is, even before that bank had opened.

Accordingly, the following routine was worked out.

(a)   11 a.m. Monday. Despatch of first carrier from Brussels.

(b)   4 to 6 p.m. Tuesday. Arrival in Hong Kong. Collection of load. Delivery to customer. Receipt of payment.

(c)   9 a.m. Wednesday. Telexing of proceeds by Ben.

(d)   9 a.m. Wednesday. Collection of proceeds by buyer in Brussels.
Conversion. Purchase of Gold.
Despatch of second carrier.

(e)   4 to 6 p.m. Thursday. Arrival in Hong Kong.

(f)   9 a.m. Friday. Proceeds of second sale back in Brussels.
Despatch of third carrier.

(g)   4 to 6 p.m. Saturday. Arrival in Hong Kong.

(h)   9 a.m. Monday. Proceeds of third sale back in Brussels, for commencement of second week.

So, one unit of capital could be turned over three times a week, which meant that if we started with twelve kilos we would be running twenty-four in six weeks. This was the theory and Ben confirmed that Hong Kong was a free currency market with no restrictions on transfer. Using this system I calculated that we could make over a quarter of a million pounds a year net. After six months of establishing ourselves in Hong Kong, where the profit margin was modest but the conditions safe, we would move into Japan where similar calculations informed me that we could make over two million pounds a year net.

Next I began to work out a day-by-day programme for each day of the first three months of operations, noting the paths of carriers through time and place, detailing the monetary transactions and showing the cash position as it would be at the end of each day in London, Brussels and Hong Kong.

Each day showed:

(a) The times of departures and arrivals of each carrier, the best flight route available plus one alternative, and his position at different times.

(b) The number of kilos that would be purchased and at what total cost, in Belgian francs and U.S. dollars.

(c) The minimum anticipated sales value, in H.K. and U.S. dollars.

(d) The deductions that Ben would need to make to pay the carrier and for his own expenses, in H.K. and U.S. dollars.

(e) The net sum that he would telex back, in H.K. and U.S. dollars and Belgian francs.

(f) The deductions that would have to be made by the buyer in Brussels before he made his purchase, to send back to London, to pay for carriers' fares at £450 a time and office expenses, in pounds sterling and Belgian francs.

(g) The balance that would be available for buying, in U.S. dollars and Belgian francs.

(h) The balance that would remain after buying.

I anticipated being able to raise only the minimum sum of £5,750 buying capital which was why our method of operation had to be so precisely detailed. Unfortunately I had filled pages and pages of foolscap paper with calculations when both British and Hong Kong currencies were devalued – unequally, leaving me with no option but to re-do them from beginning to end.

We had agreed that after a time we would operate several routes simultaneously. Up to that time we had used the word 'route' to mean an operation into a particular place, but it was decided that it should not only refer to a place but to the turning over of one unit of capital three times a week. We decided to make any frequency above this a separate operation employing new managers isolated in separate London, European and Far Eastern offices, irrespective of whether or not the final destination remained as Hong Kong. Ultimately, each route organisation would recruit its own carriers, so that if one route was blown the organisation as a whole would not be affected.

When our method of operation was fixed we had to deal with the problem of carriers. First we worked out the routine of a carrier's trip.

Three days before his departure he would be on call. The day before his departure he would be summoned to London, met somewhere and placed in a hotel. He would not be permitted to leave his room or make any telephone calls. He would not know whether he was being sent to the Middle East, the Far East, the United States, or Tierra del Fuego. He would have no knowledge of the business at all. He would be told that in general he would be carrying gold, but that quite frequently he would be carrying either pearls or diamonds, sometimes industrial chemicals, never drugs. Only on the day of departure when being seen on the train at Victoria Station would he learn that he was going to some city in Europe. This city would be changed every two to three months. At the same time he would be given the name and address of the hotel that he was to book into. He would leave London without knowing the address of our London office and with no means of contacting us. On arrival in Brussels he would be telephoned, visited and briefed by somebody, whose name he would never know but who would be in possession of a photograph and dossier on him. He would be loaded and escorted to the airport, where he would be handed his ticket, told his ultimate destination and seen on to the plane. He would not know if anyone from the organisation was travelling with him.

The other end, at Kai Tak airport, Hong Kong, he would be watched alighting from the plane by an agent (Ben initially) again possessing his photograph and dossier. He would be traced through and out of custom's hall and followed to his hotel. Once in his room he would be telephoned by a man using a pre-arranged name which could be changed for each trip. A few minutes after that, a Chinese messenger would call on him and collect. The Chinese messenger would not speak a word other than to inform him that his fee had already been delivered and was waiting for him downstairs. He would know at this point that his job was at an end, that with a pre-paid fare he could return to England when he wished.

This routine would insure that the carrier was in total ignorance of our operation. If he were caught then we would lose a load and a carrier but the organisation could not be harmed. Even if he gave the authorities my name or Ben's, it wouldn't matter as neither of us would have done anything illegal. And apart from this he knew nothing at all except for the details of his journey. (We would make sure carriers never met each other.)

The next problem was how to discourage a carrier from running off, which was bound to appear as an easy way to earn an instant ten grand or more? There were the transit stops, Frankfurt, Rome, Athens, Istanbul, Beirut, Kuwait, Cairo, Karachi, Bombay, Calcutta, Rangoon or Bangkok, at which he could get off. Of these, going blind into Cairo or any of the last five and attempting to make a sale would quickly prove disastrous. We could cut out Athens. It was Frankfurt and Rome, where he would change planes to make the Far East connection, that there was most opportunity. But for little cost he could be accompanied this far or with little aggravation a check could be made. This left Istanbul, an unsafe bet with high penalties, Kuwait, a situation unknown, and Beirut, an excellent market, which would have to be avoided as a transit stop. To limit the carriers' possibilities it was decided that before leaving London each would be made to hand over his address books, note-books, cheque books and cash. Then he would be given ten pounds for travelling expenses. These were the only physical restrictions we could make and they were far from foolproof. It was certainly not practicable to send someone with him all the way, although he could be encouraged to think that this was the case. Apart from this he would be made to understand that if he did abscond and we caught him then he would be brutally punished. 'Carriers,' said Ben, 'are the backbone of this business.' It was obvious that every consideration of risk and security revolved around them. The degree of risk would depend on whom we recruited as well as on how they were trained and briefed. We agreed to avoid recruiting those who had known connections with crime or club and gaming scenes. We would choose men with strong family ties or those with valued roots in a way of life, those who had jobs with prospects to which they were attached, with fixed property against which they might fear reprisals. We would place as much emphasis on character as on background and associations. We would have them held in awe of the kind of organisation they were working for, by creating mystery and holding them in ignorance on the one hand while inspiring them with our painstaking efficiency on the other. To help give this impression of efficiency we compiled a Manual for Carriers (*see* Appendix A, iii) – effectively a carrier's bible. At the same time we devised a deterrent which proved to be the most convincing of all. We would present the carrier with a source of income which would produce as much over a reasonable time as he would get by running off with the gold. A payment structure for carriers was worked out incorporating a bonus scheme which would reward a man making two trips a month with £7,500 a year. Along with this he could always consider the possibility that he might be promoted to assist in an administrative capacity at a salary of twelve to fourteen thousand a year.

Shortly after the devaluations which had upset my initial calculations the following letter arrived from a Mr Kuon in Hong Kong.

Dear Ben,

I thank you for your letter of the 21st instant, and am very pleased to note that you are now in a position to renew our previous transactions.

I wish to advise that I have been to Tokyo during this year already ten times for the negotiation of some big projects with the highest authorities of the Japanese Government. With my close connections there, plus former contacts, I am sure that I can offer my services better and besides you can always count on my fullest co-operation both here and in Japan. Please let me know when you have made up your decisions as I would very much like to meet you soon to finalise our arrangements.

I remain, with best regards,
Sincerely yours,

It was a valuable morale boost to us as the weeks of research had often seemed to be far removed from the actual business of gold smuggling.

But these weeks had been vital nonetheless. They had taught me facts and figures which had corroborated as well as enlarged on what Ben had originally said, and they had familiarised me with people and places. The main appeals of a gold smuggling business I now understood as follows: The profits could be large. The markets were inexhaustible. Those of Japan and Hong Kong alone were thought to absorb in the region of thirty and one hundred million dollars worth a year. The business was almost entirely legal: there would be no infringement of the law in this country, except in the initial transfer of funds out – if that proved necessary. Gold could be purchased openly on the Continent, and exported, though no resident of the U.K. could own it. The sole offence would be committed by the carrier transporting gold to the Far East with intent to avoid payment of customs duty on entry – the penalties for which varied from getting off scot free with a suspended sentence (three to six months in Hong Kong; generally eighteen months in Tokyo) to a possible fifteen years rigorous imprisonment (Korea; Vietnam). Finally, the element of risk was small. Though a loss in the first two months would wipe us out, after that it would be a small bite out of profits. Both Ben and I would be perfectly safe. Ben wouldn't even touch the gold the other end and, as for carriers, Ben insisted that they would need to be stripped for their loads to be discovered and this would only happen if they moved awkwardly or the load looked bulky. It was to avoid this that we would limit our loads to a comfortable twenty-four kilos. We were determined that our carriers should enjoy their trips as much as possible and have reason for feeling completely confident. For the carrier the appeals of the business were obvious. He would be given the opportunity to travel to far-off places which otherwise he wouldn't get to see. While working he would be living in great style in the most luxurious hotels in the world, all expenses paid. And finally there was the excitement and the adventure.

Chapter 3/Hooks in the Gullet

While researching and planning, Tania, an amazingly lovely, long-suffering and loyal girl, and I had been living in a small neatly furnished, fully serviced hotel room in the middle of Earl's Court and surviving on cheese, honey and salami sandwiches. One grand had quickly gone. Tania, the mainstay of our existence, a fact known only to her and myself, went out to work, pawned one piece after another of her small collection of jewellery and borrowed money.

We needed to work in complete uninterrupted seclusion as well as to establish the conditions of secrecy under which we would be operating in the future. So none of our friends or acquaintances were allowed to know where we were living, or have our telephone number, or know what we were doing. Only Ben's fiancée, Sandra, with whom Tania had established a great friendship, could come visiting.

Ben had a job, as a croupier, working in the evenings. His main responsibility, at this point, was for the design and production of carriers' suits. We had neither the space nor privacy to do this, so we took a flat. I had borrowed a grand against the security of another small trust which was in the process of being wound up.

The main design requirements of the suits were as follows. The suit had to be capable of withstanding the strain of at least seventy-two kilos, even though we had decided to restrict our maximum load to twenty-four. Several of Raymond's suits had broken up. To put our carriers' minds at ease we would have to be able to give impressive demonstrations of their strength. They would have to take up the least amount of space under normal clothing and be comfortable, as there would be nothing between them and the carriers' flesh. They had to have individual pockets to hold each kilo bar firmly in place. The total weight had to be distributed in such a way that the natural movement of the body would not be distorted and the pockets positioned so that the corners of the gold bars would not rub against bones or dig into flesh – a source of excruciating pain on a twenty-two-hour journey. They had to be made in various sizes.

Several experimental prototypes were made before the ideal one was found (*see* Appendix A, iv). Ben had discovered an ample supply of material from an army surplus store which could be used for shoulder straps, with a breaking strain of five hundred pounds. He also bought yards of padded nylon, extra strong nylon fabric, soft satin, foam rubber, curtain tape and cotton. While still at the experimental stage, I had purchased several pounds of lead sheetings, cut them up into pieces, melted them in a saucepan over the gas-stove, poured the molten liquid into moulds and made bars. The exact measurements of a kilo bar of gold – $\frac{1}{4}'' \times 2'' \times 4''$ – had been obtained from one of the City's bullion dealers, Samuel Montagu and Co. Ltd.

The final prototype was loaded up. The weight of lead had felt unmanageably heavy carried in the arms. Distributed evenly around the body, supported hardly at all by the shoulders but by a woman's corset worn over Ben's design, it became surprisingly unnoticeable. It was a wonder of construction. Four of us swinging from the suit could not break or rip off the straps, nor was it possible to tear off the pockets. Worn by Adam it was impossible to detect anything from his appearance.

Production began in earnest. While most of the cutting as well as tacking of the linings was done by Tania and Sandra, the actual making, the gruelling work of machine-sewing through unyielding wads of material, was done by Ben. Our target was a minimum of fifty suits.

Almost six months had passed since we had begun. Frequent exchanges had taken place between Ben and

Kuon, as well as with several other contacts in Hong Kong, all of whom were expecting shipments. Carriers, a dozen of whom had been recruited, had been promised work, flights to far-off places, days smothered by native chicks on palmed beaches, the luxury of grand hotels and magnificent earnings. All thought that we were abundantly financed, or we would never have engaged their interest. We would have to move soon or risk losing what we had built up. We needed money, and the problem of its total absence was one that would have to be solved, for the most part by myself.

The proposition I had was hardly one that could be hawked round the City or presented to my bank manager. I attempted to place an advertisement in the Personal Column of *The Times*, submitting a guardedly worded text, but this was returned with a request for a solicitor's reference and I decided not to pursue the matter. I was considering other possibilities when I met Sebastian.

'Featherington is thinking of going into the gold business,' he said. 'And apparently he's found a backer.'

This was believable. He would not have forgotten our dawn conversation with Ben and he had the contacts for raising capital. Even so, I refused to believe that he would ever reach the point of being operational; and I had a strong suspicion that he realised this himself.

A couple of nights later I telephoned him and invited him to dinner and a game of bridge. After a few polite exchanges I led him straight to our office and seemingly straight to the point.

'I know that you are interested in the gold business,' I said. 'Since I last saw you I've been working at nothing else. We have our carriers recruited, our procedures set out, sufficient capital to run a route, and customers waiting. We are due off in a few weeks.'

He sat forward eagerly.

'Do you know how much capital is required to launch this business?' I asked.

'£20,000,' he replied, quoting Ben's original figure and demonstrating that he had made no calculations himself.

'About a third of that,' I said.

Featherington, whose impecunity was well known, knew that I wouldn't be asking him for money.

'We have more than enough capital to make a start,' I continued. 'But this is not enough. There is no reason as I see it why we should ever lose a load.' I gave him my arguments on the subject. 'So one can eliminate in advance all the most likely causes of failure, except of course 'Acts of God'. A loss in the first couple of months and we would be wiped out.'

'What I am thinking is this: after the phenomenal amount of work that has gone into preparation, it would be wise to get an insurance cover of some sort.'

Featherington was no insurance broker and it was obvious that this was not what I had in mind.

'What I would like to do, therefore, is to raise the capital for at least two routes, so that if the worst comes to the worst and we are hit we would not be knocked out but able to make an instant re-start.'

'This is our first problem; not one that is vital to solve or one that is going to hold us up. The second – not one that is going to hold us up either, but one that is going to be acute when we come to the position of being able to expand – is one of people. This is why I have asked you here.'

He was staring intently at me anticipating what I was leading to. He would not accept anything menial.

'Carriers,' I said, knowing that this humble role was not what he had in mind. A hand twitched agitatedly and I imagined a shudder and deep sigh of relief as I passed quickly over the subject. 'We have plenty of these. No, they are not our problem.' I explained to him how we intended setting up each new route as an entirely independent and separate operation with Station-Managers in charge of each point and so forth. 'Now you can see what our main problem will be,' I continued. 'Finding people who are competent and whom we can trust.' The solution to this problem certainly did not lie in him. However, some gesture had to be made before there was any chance of a reciprocal one.

'Apart from the debatable point of whether or not you are capable of keeping your mouth shut, I would say you are perfect in every way for such a job. Would you be interested?'

His eyes opened wide and his face flushed with excitement.

'In what capacity?'

'As a buyer.'

'What about the Far East?' He knew the position from which he would be able to profit most: that which brought him into direct contact with customers.

'No, initially as a buyer.'

'How much will I get paid?'

I produced our 'Route Partnership Agreement for Station-Managers' (*see* Appendix A, v). One twelfth of the profits on one route was worth over fourteen grand, which was fourteen grand in excess of his earnings for each of the last five years. But it wasn't enough.

'Why a percentage of one route? What about an overall percentage? I should have an overall percentage.'

This was pushing his luck too far.

'That's absolutely out of the question. You can argue till you're blue in the face. That is the offer. Take it or leave it.'

'When do I start?' he asked.

'You start on the second route as soon as we're ready to open it.' I replied, wondering if the statement was sufficient for him to spot the crunch in it. 'That is, more or less straight away, if I am able to raise the remaining capital. Otherwise, it will come from the profits of the first route, when we have sufficient reserves to draw from – that should be in three to four months.'

That was too long for him to wait but by now he had swallowed not only the bait but the hook. If there was anything he could do to shorten this time, to keep the situation alive lest he should lose his chance, any capital to be raised to eliminate this stumbling block, then he would do it. He knew how low his own chances were of making the scene independently.

'Well, actually,' he said, after a few minutes of thought, 'I might be able to help.'

'Oh?' I exclaimed, feigning surprise.

'I've got a friend – he's got five or six thousand pounds – I know he'll be interested.'

'Oh!'

'He's gone to Stockholm for a couple of weeks. I'll give you his telephone number if you like. You can ring him.'

'Well, it would be better if we had a meeting.'

'Also, what about Goldwyn?' he suggested.

'I had thought of him,' I replied, 'but don't really know him well enough.'

'I'll arrange a meeting,' he said.

Three days later, Featherington telephoned.

'I've spoken with Goldwyn. He's interested. I think he'll put in two and a half thousand.'

'Very good.' I said. 'Ask him to come to dinner. Does he play bridge? Good. Arrange it for tomorrow night.'

'Looks like we have an investment consultant in the City who is going to back us', I said to Ben.

'Yeah?' He was at his endless labouring on the sewing machine, speckled and half entangled in cotton thread and stuffing from the bodies of the suits.

'Yeah! Remember Goldwyn?'

Goldwyn, despite his youth, was like an old world Victorian curiosity, and had been a source of wonder and delight to Ben ever since he had encountered him at one of our games.

'Fantastic. Really? Fantastic. Punting again! We'll have an official quotation on the stock exchange yet.'

Featherington was certainly proving co-operative. He had

B

been hustled, yet somehow, because it was the way we had decided to work, I would eventually have to honour my word to him.

He arrived early in the evening, Goldwyn a couple of hours afterwards. Ben was still working on the machine and Adam was loaded for a demonstration.

Goldwyn was shown around, then given a demonstration. I took him to our office and was amazed to discover he was not interested to read our procedures, or to go into any details of the business, or to examine my calculations, or indeed to enquire into any matters of policy. All he wanted to know was our estimate of yearly profits and the percentage interest offered per grand invested. Yes, he said, he would invest two and a half thousand, which was all he had to spare at that moment. We had come to an agreement within ten minutes.

'Aren't there any points you would like me to go over?' I asked.

'It's a matter of faith,' he said. This was very encouraging.

'When do you need the money?' he asked.

'In about six weeks,' I replied.

'Fair enough. Let me know exactly when you're off. Meanwhile I'll instruct my broker to sell the necessary stocks.'

'I'll type out the main points of our agreement for clarification and to avoid any possible misunderstanding in the future. I'll post it to you in the morning.'

'Is Featherington-Smythe involved with you?'

'No,' I said. 'He's not. Thinks he might be, but isn't.'

Ben was working at this time for the manager of a discotheque called Shirak who I saw as a possible backer. So after gradually informing Ben that we needed a little more money I suggested that he approach him. Eventually he did.

'What did you say to him?' I asked.

'Well, I approached him in a very indirect fashion. We were at the bar. It was crowded. I just said I had a proposition. He told me he had a hundred a night but he'd listen to it. It had better be good. He'd see me again tonight.'

There was usually nothing timid about Ben; but Shirak was his employer and Ben's sole means of existence.

'Why don't I arrange a meeting, the three of us? You can talk facts and figures better.'

'Okay. Invite him here tomorrow afternoon. What shall we offer him?'

'I'll leave it up to you,' he said.

'What's his peculiar nationality? I always forget?'

'Sherkasian. They're South Russian Arabs. Not Kurds. And they don't like to be called Arabs either.'

Shirak arrived. He swaggered in, giving the impression of Al Capone as portrayed by Edward G. Robinson, as though he was too tall for the part. A warm handshake and his face and eyes opened into a smile.

Ben had already disclosed the nature of the business, and was convinced that he would be interested. Particularly well-known on the London club scene he was the last kind of person we wanted, but time was short.

He sat down on the bed in front of my make-do desk. I outlined briefly the main principles of the business and invited him to go into any details he wished. The degree of his interest was soon obvious and he spent a great deal of time reading slowly and seeming to digest carefully our 'Carriers Procedures'. It had occurred to me that perhaps he couldn't read English very well, though he had no difficulty in speaking it. His reading was punctuated by questions and loud exclamations. We soon realised that he was as determined to make an impression on us as we were on him. He became quite excited and enthusiastic about the idea then tried to pull it to pieces. But despite his merciless assault he found nothing that had been overlooked.

I took an instant liking to him. He opened his whole personality, reacting instantly, holding back nothing, his force vibrating powerfully.

'Well what's the deal? Where do I fit in?'

'You don't,' I said.

'Oh!' he said, paralysed, until he interpreted the expression on my face and beamed broadly.

'Well our position is this,' I began. 'We require altogether £7,000 capital to launch this business. We already have half of it. We need the other half. If you can provide us with the other half we'll offer you twenty-five per cent of the profits net on the first route we open. This should represent a return on capital of over 1,000 per cent per annum.'

'What do you mean, the first route?' he questioned.

I explained to him, pointing out also that the agreement would be for one year only.

'I'm not interested,' he said.

'Oh!' I was slightly amazed.

'It's not the figure. It's not the money. It's the principle.'

'What principle?' I asked.

'Either I'm going to be in with you or I'm not going to be in with you.'

'Twenty-five per cent is a very good offer. In fact it's ridiculous.'

'What do you take me for?' he asked, becoming very angry, looking hurt, disappointed and insulted.

'I don't understand,' I said.

Ben interrupted. 'He doesn't understand.' He looked at Shirak, putting his hand on his shoulders. Then he turned to me. 'What he means is that he's either completely in with us as a full partner or not at all. He doesn't want any of this route business.'

'I'm with you. You've taken me by surprise. We have never thought about having a partner. That's different. We'll think it over; it's an idea. Ben is going to be running the Far East side. It will be too much for me to handle the

European and London sides. Yes, it's quite an idea. You could run the London office. I'm inclined to accept on the spot, however, we'll talk it over together and meet tomorrow. Okay?'

Shirak returned to his original happy self; and left, after another firm and warm shaking of hands.

'What do you think?' Ben asked.

'I definitely feel inclined to trust him.'

'Oh, you can trust him all right. He's never done anybody up in his life. And who else can you say the same about on his kind of scene?'

'It's a big decision. We have to think seriously, because there'll be no going back. We'll be stuck with him for the rest of our lives. The money bit doesn't matter. You're not greedy, I'm not greedy. There's enough for everybody. Well, he's used to running people – got his own boys – we don't want any Arabs as carriers though.'

'Definitely not. They'd get sussed out straight away.'

'There was too much for him to digest on one sitting. He was confused. Still it took me six months. He's hooked all right.'

'If we have him, we have him all the way down the line. If he doesn't gamble all his money away at the club, he'll always put more in. That's good insurance.'

Following the recruitment of more carriers, and one other organiser we would be ready to start.

Chapter 4/'Is this Candid Camera?'

We had fifteen carriers but needed thirty to forty, and quickly, as at least a month was necessary for training.

Shirak, who was now a full partner, would not approve. The thought of carriers he didn't know (even those we already had), carrying his investment, horrified him, so it was decided not to tell him. If he did find out we would say that the decision to run the ad had been taken before he joined.

The following advertisement was inserted:

'Interesting and remunerative part-time work, with travel, offered to adventurous and well educated young man.'

Tania was given the job of finding and hiring suitable facilities in a large hotel. She found a suite in the Cumberland at Marble Arch, and booked it in the name of James Summers.

I worked out a standard letter inviting applicants to an interview and another for rejections, then worked out a method of interviewing them which would enable us to find out whether the idea of carrying gold interested those who interested us. This was difficult since we would have to be absolutely sure of them before giving them any idea of what we were doing.

A month earlier, we had recruited a carrier, Paul Cotton, whom we had discovered through a friend of Tania's. He was a hairdresser by profession, but preferred to be regarded as an out-of-work actor and had a pilot's licence (produced on request). In appearance he bore a phenomenal likeness to Gregory Peck.

Filling in the usual detailed forms, he noted his main interests in life as 'buying and restoring semi-vintage cars', adventure and travel. He had brought two documents, signed by a late Prime Minister of Australia and bearing his seal, requesting whatever country to extend the maximum courtesies to his personal friend, Paul's father, and any members of his immediate family while they were on a visit. Even if these documents were forgeries, they were impressive!

On one occasion he had brought a distorted oval shaped lump of gold out of his pocket.

'Where's that from?'

'My own mine,' he said.

It was a small mine that had been left to him by his father and which they had worked at week-ends.

After several meetings, he seemed to be reliable and have sufficient common sense, and therefore I told him that I was intending to use him in a more administrative capacity; that along with Adam I would train him to run our London office and despatch carriers; and later, even to recruit them. Though Shirak reacted violently to the idea of delegating work, responsibility or authority, he would have to come round to accepting the principle. Meanwhile, Paul would attend the interview.

We had over two hundred replies to our advertisement, one consisting of the single sentence 'I'm your man', and another containing a fifteen-page printed booklet of curriculum vitae, which obliged us to deduce that what we had to offer was not quite what the gentleman was looking for, and lead us to wonder what strange twists of fate had prevented him from heading half-a-dozen multi-million pound companies. One applicant wrote that he had just returned from prison in Poland and was now prepared to do anything legal. Another that he was an Indian, had been a tight-rope walker in Calcutta, boiler-stoker on a tramp steamer, drummer in a San Francisco band, lumberjack in Canada, that he had written a book and been all over the world . . . and would we please not be put off by any of these facts as 'I ham heducated'. Two applications were from officers in the RAF both of whom were about to give up their commissions. Several were freelance writers – some for television. One had several 'thrillers' to his credit; another had written guide books to Bangkok, Japan and Cambodia. Most, to our surprise had professional qualifications.

All were rejected save thirty who were invited to attend interviews and appointments were made.

Present were Tania, Ben's girl Sandra, Ben, Paul Cotton and myself. One of the reasons for having the two girls there was to de-sinisterize the proceedings.

We quickly arranged an accept-reject signal. If I thought a candidate was suitable I would light a cigarette, then put the cigarettes back on the table with the lighter to the left of the cigarettes. If Ben reached an opinion on the candidates suitability before I did then he would make the signal. If an acceptance signal was made by one of us then the other would decide whether he agreed, if so he would deliver the punch line: 'What would you say if you were asked to carry gold?' We intended to interrogate them thoroughly, politely avoiding any questions on the nature of the job advertised. If the candidate was to be rejected he would be given a story about taking coach tours around the Continent.

The following is Ben's account of the proceedings:

'Starting from my arrival at the interview suite: I entered the room, slightly late, seated myself at table at partner's left hand. Partner appears trifle huffy with me, but then gives me full benefit of his most charming smile – signalling his forgiveness of my morning's sins: 'I'm going to leave the opening chat to you,' he says. Very, very kind, I can't help thinking. Very slight panicky feeling at thought of opening interview with troupe of bright public-schooled young men most of whom must be brimming over with expertise. At this point Tania ushers in bloke No. 1.

'He sits, accepts coffee, emanating extreme nervousness, in turn bolstering my own sagged confidence one hundred per cent.

'With gentle help this young man regaled the company with his current occupation which, I can't recall exactly, but he was I think working for a branch of the Government responsible for the control and supply of waste paper baskets, bicycle clips and used string, to East Durham Urban Council, or some such! It occurred to me 'Obvious rejection' but in the meantime had forgotten which signal from partner was 'reject' and so I suspect had partner who suddenly put both cigarettes and lighter in pocket, destroying signal apparatus, giving at same time encouraging smile and unnecessarily sharp tap on ankles. Young man given diplomatic elbow. If nothing else, he served some purpose to us as ice-breaker.

'Quick whispered conference at table. Signal system perfected. Ankle tapping discouraged.

'I cannot recall too well the sequence of appointments. The second, I think, survived the first five minutes.

'Enter the third.

'He was asked his past occupations. Yes, he would consider something slightly unorthodox.

'Would you care to read this and give your reactions?' asked partner brightly. The fellow began to read. Gradually, as he became aware of the portent of what he was reading, he seemed to find some difficulty in sitting comfortably in his seat – his fidgeting now accompanied by furtive glances over top of book. When finished, cleared throat and asked: 'Is this really serious?'

' "Oh yes," assured partner, who had now come very much to life and proceeded to answer searing questions from prospective carrier such as "Won't the gold be visible beneath clothes?" and so forth, with brilliant accuracy.

'Complicated signals flash around the room, the product

of which is that Paul with winning smile rises, almost curtsies, quickly divests himself of clothes, exposing now rose-patterned corset, suspenders still attached. With difficulty and some redness of face, corset rolls down, exposing to no one's surprise but the now very glassy-eyed young man a pastel blue nylon sort of mini-skirt with serried rows of pockets from the top of which peep almost coyly – bars of lead.

'The male model who sheepishly shuffles towards door, adjusting his "fly" as he does so. At model's exit applicant makes tentative, and I think hopeful, enquiry, "Is this Candid Camera?" Gravely assured it is not, his curiosity now excited beyond the just receded feeling of fear for either his mind or limb, he accepts further refreshment – and is hooked.

'At later hour, enter very cool young man in very "with-it" Carnaby Street inspired but not tailored clothes, with matching hair, and exuding extreme confidence in voice and movement. Remember him as being very very witty and first-rate material. Having read procedure book, copped the model routine, etc., with in fact great aplomb, no eyelid batting, legs still elegantly crossed, cigarette still dangling, in fact with such an impressive show of indifferent cool that one almost expected him to say "Paint me all over with green stripes and I'll still look slightly bored". He says: "Of course, I'll have to be particularly careful there as so many of my friends are members of the jet set." A very naughty one to drop!

'The next applicant was a nervous young Scotsman. He read the procedure book with a look as if it contained message that his mother would never again give him shortcake for tea or butter his scones or take him to see X films – and I would lay money that she'd bade him "Nay go near Soho and all they turrrribel London wenches. Ye mon, save yurr baudy fo yon bonnie wee Maggie Slot." Here he now sits in the Cumberland Hotel with a bird the tops of whose thighs he can see, pouring him coffee and being invited to travel east bearing gold and his mind racing how to explain to Maggie it wasn't selling brushes and praying his boss will never find out that he wasn't taking his day off to go to his Uncle Hamish's funeral. When his train roared through Grimsby he would make up his mind to burn all his adventure books when he got home.

'What do you imagine could really have been going through a fellow's mind during, say, the fifteen minutes of exposure he has undergone since arriving at what he would naturally have assumed to be some sort of rep job?'

Ben had had us in tears at the time of these interviews. We were rolling around on the floor and it was an incredible strain to resume our formal poses before the next applicant came along. Nobody had taken time off to join in a panto-mime and we were engaged in serious business and had to put an effective image across. Ben's actual performance could not have been more controlled, serious, or suitably impressive.

Recruiting carriers in this way was surprisingly effective. Only a handful of those selected for interview failed to attend and only three of these were rejected. The advertisement had put us in touch with a fund of potentially good material, but considerable research into background was going to be necessary. Each candidate still considered acceptable after the second interview would be the exhaustively checked.

Second interviews followed immediately. Different places were found and only two applicants were interviewed at any one place, and separately. This was to avoid the consequences of possible come-backs. The days were a Wednesday, a Thursday and a Friday and as we were only a few days off moving out of our Earl's Court flat, two of the interviews were held there.

On the Saturday we had a visitor. A man who explained

he was interested in a job in the import and export line. Could I tell him a little bit about it?

'You must have come to the wrong address,' I said, but he was insistent.

'I'm not living here myself,' I continued, 'but as far as I know there is nobody living here who's in that line of business. I think there's only a doctor and some bird working in one of the Scandinavian embassies.'

He still showed no interest in going so I closed the door on him. One of our interviewees had obviously been talking.

The following morning I had a telephone call from our latest investor, not Shirak, but a friend of both Adam and mine who had agreed to put up one grand. He didn't sound at all worried and told me that he knew everything must be under control but . . . did we know that we were featured in that day's issue of the *Sunday Times*?

'Naturally', I said, 'we do. We decided to blow our own scene. But don't worry. Everything is perfectly under control.'

'I thought it was,' he said.

Such a show of confidence was reassuring but I wanted to know what he was talking about.

'Look. I've got somebody with me at the moment,' I said, 'I'll call you back later.'

'Fine,' he said, 'I'm terribly intrigued.'

So was I, but not from such a comfortable position. Goldwyn, who had assured us of two and a half grand, would also read the article; while if Shirak came across it, he would go into an hysterical rage.

'SECRETS OF A HOTEL ROOM AND THE MEN WITH THE GOLDEN CORSETS', it began. 'International gold smugglers are hiring British Passport holders to wear corsets lined with gold sheeting on flights from Geneva to Hong Kong. For each trip carriers are paid £200. Potential carriers are being recruited brazenly through advertisements placed in the Situations Vacant column of *The Times*. Two applicants told the *Sunday Times* last week that they had replied to a box number and about a week later . . . ' – So far, nothing damaging; and it was difficult to see how anything could be.

'The story is now taken up by a young university graduate who has already made two trips for the smugglers on the "Geneva run".' A phenomenal performance in two days! ' 'Before I set out on my first trip,` he said, 'I was told that if I was caught, the sentence would be three months behind bars. I've never done anything illegal before and I kept wondering whether I really needed the £200 so badly.' It had seemed like he had needed an instant tenner a good deal more. 'I was told to pick up an envelope at the Swissair counter at Heathrow Airport. As I drove myself to the terminal I can remember thinking to myself, "It's too late to want to become a clerk in an office somewhere".' With a university degree? Readers' hearts must have been torn out. 'My instructions were to go to the Hotel Beau Rivage in Geneva, where I would be contacted. Twenty-four hours later a slightly built Frenchman presented himself. Then began the corset fitting. The Frenchman lifted the harness out of his case with the tenderness of a priest about to robe a novice.' I read that sentence twice – he was certainly on some kind of trip. 'My instructions were to go to Hong Kong on a non-stop BOAC flight.' (This would have been a problem – there isn't one.) 'Although I can't prove it, I suspect a more senior member of the gang was on the plane to keep an eye on me.'

And so he rolled on with the details of his fantasy.

The article continued: 'As the *Sunday Times* representative left the premises [previously referred to], the man who said he was a final year medical student photographed their car from a balcony.'

I had always said that any information leaked by a carrier could do us no harm and this was the test. It was just unfortunate that it happened at a time when we were completely dependent on our investors and their confidence in us.

I telephoned the investor and explained to him about the interviews at the Cumberland. He was surprised to hear this as he imagined the story was a complete invention and even that we had put it in ourselves. 'No.' I said, 'We got blown. But we expected to be. Journalists as you know, regularly scrutinize the columns for leads and we were quite prepared to have one of them coming along. You could say that this was being a bit over-cool, but we simply cannot be blown by any press story. Anyway, as you said, the situation is well under control. I've organised a second article which is going to show the whole thing up as a hoax.' He was satisfied.

Next I telephoned Goldwyn. He hadn't seen the story. 'Thought I'd give you a buzz to put you in the picture.' Goldwyn was satisfied too.

I decided not to tell Shirak. The chances of him reading the *Sunday Times* or any newspaper were minute.

The only problem left was to arrange for a hoax story. We would tell our carriers that we had blown the scene ourselves to kill all potential stories dead. Indeed, it could be extremely useful as it would certainly remove any doubts about the pregnability of the organisation.

A couple of days later the following headlines appeared in a daily newspaper: 'GOLD SMUGGLING JOBS WERE JUST A JOKE, CLAIMS TANIA'. It bore a photograph of her, with one of the 'suits' slung over her shoulders, with a bar of lead in one hand, and a policeman behind her. 'Tania . . . admitted yesterday that she advertised for employees who were later asked if they would smuggle gold to The Far East. But Tania, a 23-year-old Chelsea girl said "We were not serious. We did it for a laugh . . . One of the men interviewed has claimed that he smuggled gold to the Far East. We know who the man was – but he certainly did not travel on our behalf . . . I suppose it's time that all the would-be smugglers know we were having them on." '

As an explanation this was much more convincing than the truth. People would find it difficult to believe that real smugglers would advertise for staff in a national paper.

The day after, in another newspaper a further story appeared: 'WHY I TRIED TO FIND GOLD SMUGGLERS'. This had come from me. 'I was obtaining information for a book.'

The original article in the *Sunday Times* had mentioned the address of our flat which could only have come from one of the two applicants who had been interviewed there and as I was extremely grateful to this daily for giving me advance publicity on my book, I had given them the names and addresses of the two gentlemen suggesting that they might have some interesting quotes. One was guilty and the other would have to be blown anyway. It was of no interest to us, which was which. Thirty-year-old Mr Michael Hawes of Perryvale, Forest Hill, London, was interviewed: 'He was "not amused" when he heard Mr Knowles' claim that he had not been serious.'

Punch, a week later, had the last word on the subject:

'The *Sunday Times* fearlessly exposed a gold racket which had been run with the aid of personal advertisements in *The Times*. Good to find LORD THOMSON OF FLEET keeping such a watchful eye on himself.

'It is difficult to believe what one reads in the newspapers these days!'

Chapter 5/Catastrophe

Our head office was in a semi-luxurious flat on the second floor of a large Georgian house a couple of minutes walk from Hyde Park. Shirak's flat in Queen's Gate, referred to as Q on procedure files, was being used for suit-production and meeting carriers, while my flat in Courtfield Gardens was the communications centre. Any correspondence sent from Hong Kong to Brussels or vice versa would be sent to Courtfield Gardens and subsequently re-addressed.

We were nearly ready to start when an utterly catastrophic event took place which rendered obsolete almost every calculation I had made over the past months and threatened to put us out of business before we had begun. Overnight, the entire structure of the gold market, which had been virtually the same for the past thirty-five years, changed. During this time the official international price had been fixed at thirty-five dollars an ounce. Now an 'open' or 'free' market had been created. (This is fully analysed in Appendix A, vi). The buying price, instead of being static, could now jump up and down, daily perhaps, anywhere between thirty-five and forty-five dollars an ounce. This meant that it was now theoretically possible to make a loss smuggling. We might buy gold at forty dollars, but by the time it arrived in Hong Kong the price might be less. It also meant that we could not plan or forecast as we had done, and that the system which I had devised to make the maximum use of the minimum amount of capital, building up from a load of twelve kilos to twenty-four and turning an initial £5,700 into a hundred thousand in a few months, was now worthless. And worse: with an increase in the price our initial buying capital would have to be more, and now we did not have enough. There seemed no possibility of raising more.

48

To make matters worse, Ben had recently informed me that Shirak was in serious financial difficulties, having lost a fortune gambling. So far he had advanced us a thousand pounds to cover immediate expenses and unfortunately I had not pressed him for the further six that he had promised. My reason for this was that Shirak was very sensitive about his status in the partnership. He was able to contribute very little, despite every encouragement given him, and it would have been an unwise move to have allowed it to appear that he was only required for his money. Although this was true, we considered relationships important and Shirak, as a friend and character, was very much liked.

If we did not start soon we would lose everything and everybody and be worse than 'back to square one' because we would have lost goodwill and be considerably in debt.

At around this time I met Karbi, Shirak's brother, who had recently arrived from Venezuela. One evening, while Shirak was at the club, and with Tania curled up on the couch sleeping, Karbi and I settled down to a game of chess. While playing, he related his life's story.

He had arrived in the States, broke, and worked his way through university. He had obtained several degrees and was now an engineering consultant with a large American company. He was about to take up an appointment as head of their marketing operations in North Africa and the Middle East. He had won amateur boxing and wrestling championships. He was devoted to his wife and kids, who were at present in Norway. The facts which he related to support the image he was trying to put across may have been disputable, but he did impress me with his intelligence and I felt that he probably was a competent organisation man.

He certainly knew that we were involved in something with his brother, but he had no means of knowing what, unless Shirak had confided in him – which we were assured he hadn't, or unless he had been snooping and Shirak had been careless enough to leave the door of our suit-production room unlocked.

'The only reason I'm here,' he said, 'is to help my brother.'

Shirak had been in hospital after a serious accident in his E-type Jaguar, from which it had taken six hours to cut him out. Shirak's several escapes from death were phenomenal.

'If he had asked me to come here, I would never have come. There was no other member of the family here. His father would have nothing to do with him. My mother begged me to come. There was no one to look after his business, which was losing money and going to pieces. I'm fed up. It's cost me money, brought trouble, caused ridiculous scenes, and has been thoroughly inconvenient. I'd sworn I'd never come again, yet here I am. And there's nothing anyone can do for him. He's got no sense and won't listen to advice. He throws all his money away gambling, and that's the last he'll ever have. And he treats me like another of his slaves. And for what? To work all night in a lousy club from eleven to seven in the morning! For what? To be an unpaid employee who works twice as hard as anyone else and get treated as if I were any son of a bitch?'

There wasn't much brotherly love between them. Rather, a fierce rivalry. At the age of three Shirak had crept up behind him and smashed a rock over his head. It seemed that his approach had been the same ever since.

The following evening, we continued our chess. Karbi disclosed that he knew exactly what we were doing. He also realised that we were having difficulties, though neither Ben nor I had uttered so much as a word to him. He went hard to work on a line which appeared afterwards to have been well worked out.

He was flattering. He told me how the rarest thing in life was to find a suitable partner and, constantly, how he could find one in me. 'You and I could run a great operation together,' he said. What kind of operation, he didn't mention, though it was obvious what he was leading up to. When he had laid his cards on the table I told him outright that whether he worked with us or not was a matter solely between him and his brother. I had no intention of getting involved in a family dispute and I told him. However, we did need a European Station-Manager urgently and it was possible that he was in a position to put up some capital.

'Okay, I'll ask my brother,' Karbi said.

By the following evening he had made no approach.

'Wouldn't it be better if you made the approach?' he asked.

'No, it would not.'

By the following evening he had still made no approach.

'I'll wait,' he said. 'Soon my brother is going to need me. And he'll come running. He needs me now more than he imagines.'

The following afternoon I arrived at Queen's Gate, from the London Office, to talk to Ben and see how the last stages of suit-production were coming along. Tania, Ben, and Karbi were there. Suddenly Shirak stormed into the room, obviously in a seething rage.

'Out,' he ordered Karbi, 'Go into the other room.' Tania discreetly followed.

'What's going on behind my back?' Shirak said, directing the question at Ben. 'Do I or do I not count in this damn business?'

'Nothing's going on behind your back.' Ben replied calmly.

'What about my brother then?' he roared. 'What about my brother then?!'

He was trying desperately to control himself but failing.

'What about him?' asked Ben, 'What's all this about?'

I remained in the background. It was obvious what had happened.

'You've invited him to come into this business, haven't you? You've been scheming behind my back. You're a bloody traitor, aren't you?'

He was breathing in and out noisily, spitting saliva with each word. He raised his right hand as if he was going to smash it into Ben's face. This was no light threat. Shirak was a man of immense strength with legendary resources of brute energy.

'Rubbish!' I interrupted. 'Complete rubbish!'

He made no recognition of having heard and didn't look at me.

'Well,' he continued, still to Ben, 'Is it true or isn't it?'

He waited for a moment for an answer before continuing. 'You bloody traitor. I'll deal with you.'

'No, it's not true,' Ben replied, refusing to be riled.

'It's quite definitely not true.' I supported.

He turned to me for the first time, his fierce eyes staring threateningly.

'Your brother was told quite clearly by me that if he wanted to come into the business, then it was a matter between you and him – and not Ben and myself. I made it quite clear that I didn't want to be mixed up in a family business.'

When I had finished speaking he turned back to Ben.

'Were you talking with my brother?'

'Of course I was talking with your brother,' Ben replied.

'And why the bloody hell were you discussing business with him in the first place? You bloody traitor! I'll fix you.'

Then he went beserk.

The low Regency-style coffee table was the first to go. He jumped on it. It collapsed. He tried furiously to wrench one of the legs off to use as a weapon but lost patience. He rose from the floor and, seeing another table, attacked that, turning its contents on the floor, including the sewing machine along with pins and material that had been placed on top, dropped whatever idea had been in his head and stormed round the room, roaring threats and insults and ripping everything off the walls. Returning to the second table he tried to rip its legs off. One of these would certainly have made a lethal weapon, but once again he left his task unfinished. He stumbled over to the sewing machine, picked that up and hurled it in the direction of Ben, missing but making a deep gash in the plaster beside him. He returned to the table. With one wrench, he uprooted a leg and approached Ben, who had remained motionless throughout, menacingly.

'I'm going to kill you. You traitor.'

Ben didn't move an inch, neither raising a hand to defend himself, nor flickering an eyelid.

'This is ridiculous,' I said, and left.

From the adjoining room further thundering and roaring could be heard as they verbally fought it out.

Such performances occurred frequently with Shirak but this was the first time they had touched our business. Eventually he left Ben and went to the kitchen, where he remained sulking for the next three hours.

A few days later, Karbi left for Norway to see his wife and kids. Both brothers had sworn never to speak to each other again.

'In a few days', Karbi had said, as he stood at the doorway, 'he'll be down on his knees to me begging me to help him. You'll see.'

'And if he does, you'll be back in a shot,' I told him.

'Never again,' he said solemnly, 'never.'

Chapter 6/In Spite of the Odds

Shirak had indeed lost all his money and he was no longer an asset but a severe liability: unreliable, dangerously uncontrollable, and destructive, seeking to impose his will on all occasions with a dismally limited intelligence.

We were paralysed unless we increased our capital, and the exact day of our departure, which had been fixed two months earlier and for which all necessary arrangements had been made, was ten days off: the day of the despatch of the first carrier. Before this, Ben had to go to Hong Kong and I to Brussels.

Despite the state of things, I absolutely refused to entertain any thought of marking time. We would depart on the fixed date, on time, whatever the situation. Accordingly, I despatched Ben, while Tania took a plane to Malta until things were more organised, and, though it was insufficient, I called in the promised capital. Adam booked the tickets for the first dozen carriers, including his own. He would be the first off, so that he could return immediately to prepare and despatch the others. He had responded to training admirably. Paul was brought round to the London Office, for the first time, to be prepared to relieve Adam during his absence.

I was gambling on the possibility that Ben might, as he had suggested, be able to raise a loan in Hong Kong; or that I could persuade Shirak to reconsider Karbi, who might have some cash; or that in the days remaining something might turn up . . . Featherington-Smythe's original backer was still a possibility. He had not been contacted, being still out of the country, but he was expected shortly.

'You have to contact Karbi,' I said to Shirak.

'Never,' he replied.

The following letter arrived from Ben, headed: 'Room

1225, The Mandarin Hotel'. It read: 'I was met on my arrival by my good friend Kuon and after bathing, etc., was able to get straight to work. Let me first of all completely reassure you of the extreme ease of passage through all formalities at journey's end. The only question that I was asked was 'Did you have a nice trip sir?'; then I was waved through. I shall be seeing the bank manager in the morning to arrange transfers. I have already arranged a completely secure method of 'pick-up' with co-operation of my good friends. Briefly, the situation regarding our proposed second major route [Tokyo] will entail my going up there to work out details; but the important point is that I am assured of customers there. I will relay information regarding all other possible markets as soon as I am able. My own feelings now toward our initial vital period are completely relaxed and one hundred per cent confident. All our sales force have to do is follow instructions to the letter. Sincerely.'

There was no mention of money.

I showed this letter to Shirak.

'All's set; we're off, then,' he beamed in a blaze of delight. Money to him was an abstract.

'We're off nowhere,' I said, and it took the remainder of the day to convince him that the inclusion of Karbi was our only chance.

But Shirak's acceptance was only half the solution. Would Karbi himself accept? The business of communicating and negotiating with him was left up to me.

'I never want to see or speak to him again,' said Shirak. This would be difficult. If Karbi accepted, he would be stationed in Brussels, and an easy flow of communications between one office and another would be vital.

I telephoned Karbi in Norway and we came to an agreement. This was ratified by Shirak. Karbi would invest all the money he had, which was very little, and until knowing on the spot how the new open market was behaving we would not know whether we had sufficient. It was disappointing that after months of the most careful precision planning we were now involved in a gamble.

I arranged to meet Karbi in Brussels.

I was driven to Dover by Belman, one of Shirak's henchmen, who was to be tried as an assistant, in an Austin Healey Sprite. We were escorted all the way by a jubilant Shirak and a riotous troup of Sherkasians in their E-type Jags, none of whom knew what the hell was going on. Belman and I caught the midnight ferry for Ostend.

I checked into the hotel Atlanta dead tired and awoke late the next morning to the uncheering headlines, 'LONDON GOLD PRICE REACHES NEW PEAK'. The explanation given was that on top of an already unstable market there was a U.S. Tax Surcharge Bill pending. The gold market was now the subject of every economic and political breeze. The price in Europe was now $40 an ounce; that in Hong Kong was $42.50. A $2.50 margin would just be sufficient to cover our overheads, but we needed a $3.50 margin to build up to a load of twenty-four kilos – at which level, price fluctuations could not seriously affect us.

I wrote to Ben: 'Even if the current situation does not improve over the next few days, I am sending out "L2" as scheduled.' 'L2' was the code which informed him of the name of the carrier, the day of his arrival and the time of his arrival – thus eliminating much risk in communications. 'It is better that we get the machinery working even if we make a loss, as there are too many people dependent on us whom we cannot without serious damage to goodwill keep waiting. We must play for time for a decrease in the price this end or an increase at yours – also, with the chance of raising more capital. "L2", Mandarin'. Ben had already moved to Repulse Bay, which I could see from the map was on the non-city side of Hong Kong Island.

I went to the bank where I had already opened an account and where the gold buyer had his offices. Ben had recently paid a visit to him, to make contact. I had to find out if it was possible to take delivery of the gold early in the morning, load the carrier and get him to the airport not later than 11.45 a.m., in time to catch his plane. An easy matter, it seemed. In point of fact it was not.

Due to the fact that the price of gold in Brussels was fixed in relation to the Zurich and London markets, the price for the morning would not be known until about 10.15. No dealings would be done on the previous day's price, in case it had risen. Also, gold had to be paid for in cash. 'It doesn't matter if you're a millionaire,' the broker told me. In Belgium it had to be paid for in Belgian francs. Initially we would not have cash floating around; we would be dependent on our transfers; and these transfers would arrive from Hong Kong in U.S. dollars. The procedure, then, would be as follows:

At 9.00 a.m. I would go to the first floor of the bank to its Foreign Department to check that the cash had been cabled. I would obtain a note to that effect and present it to the cashier downstairs, who would credit our external dollar account. A transfer would be made from this to our Belgian franc account, from which I would make the withdrawal. I would then contact the dealer on the second floor and accompany him to the Ritz-style luxury of the vaults, where the transaction would take place. If all went smoothly I would be able to leave the bank before 10.45. Belman or Karbi would assist me. We would have an hour in which to drive to his hotel, load him, and drive him to the airport. Would this be possible?

We made three dummy runs and decided that it would be.

The despatch of Adam, the first carrier, was utterly straightforward. Karbi and I purchased fourteen kilos of gold, costing about £7,500, the day before his arrival by boat and train from London. With cash in hand there had been no problem of transfer.

I wrote a note for Adam to deliver to Ben, addressing it to a Monsieur Claude Garnet, and scribbled the following coded instructions on it: L2Z14KXFLZ150. Ben would break this down as follows: L2-14K-FL-150. He would know from this that Adam ought to have fourteen kilos on him; that he himself was to telex the full proceeds of sale back to Brussels, making no deductions for his own expenses; and that Adam was to be paid £150 of his fee, the balance of which he would receive in London.

After seeing Adam onto the plane, I arranged for the following telegram to be sent from London, timed to arrive in Hong Kong a couple of hours after Adam: 'PATRICIA SERIOUSLY ILL STOP DADDY'. This was a signal to come back, and it could be used to explain his immediate exit.

Adam was despatched on a Monday morning. On Wednesday, the morning when the next carrier was to be despatched, I arrived at the bank at nine o'clock to discover that the proceeds of sale on Adam's fourteen kilos had not arrived. This was serious. Our system was nothing without a direct and instant telex link. The despatch of carrier 'L3' therefore had to be cancelled, and the procedures for instant telexing established.

Eventually the transfer arrived thirty-six hours late. It had not come direct to Brussels but via The Swiss Banking Corporation in Zurich, as Ben's Hong Kong bank had no link with my bank. Ben explained the problem in a letter. 'It is not possible for a bank to telex money immediately to any other bank simply by paying in the money and paying the telex charge. Also this cannot be done from Hong Kong through London, as to transfer our amount of dollars there three times per week direct would jeopardise us without a bona fide business here. Since devaluation and the pressure on the U.S. dollar, the money market here is no longer "free" – in the sense of sending money out of Hong Kong and not having to account for its coming and going. The money must be transferred through New York.'

It took one week of intense activity to solve this technical problem. The money was not transferred through New York. It arrived direct.

'L4' had been despatched on the Friday of the first week. The price situation had not improved. I sent the following note to Ben: 'We definitely have insufficient capital with which to operate with the price situation between here and Hong Kong as it is. Therefore do everything in your power to prepare for "second major route" [Tokyo] at earliest. Also prepare for the despatch of carriers into Singapore, Djakarta, Manila, and Bangkok.

'Regarding the second major route, I want to know about customer and payments situations, as well as Kuon's personal experience and opinions. What is the exact nature of your relationship with him and his financial interest in us? What commission has he been promised?' •

During the second week, carriers 'L5', 'L6' and 'L7' were despatched. All the transfers arrived promptly. The carriers confirmed that their entrance had been easy. By mid-week however, the price had reached the peak of $41.70 an ounce, without any compensating adjustment in Hong Kong. Unless we moved temporarily into an alternative market we would be in serious financial trouble.

Ben replied by return.

'As for Hong Kong, the price situation is very disappointing, but the system itself now seems to be functioning perfectly. This route is so safe, it's wonderful.

'Have contacts with customers in Singapore and Bangkok but I will have to go there to arrange delivery and payment. I'll be a day in each. This will not interfere with the routine of carriers arriving here. In case I'm delayed, I will leave details of the next arrival with Kuon – who can be trusted absolutely.

'As for my relationship with Kuon: nobody could be more helpful. He has accepted £25 per load as commission and he earns it, believe me. He accepts no payment for the first six weeks and we can pay him up to date in six months' time, if we wish.

'The Tokyo question is as follows – we have customers there. However, it is not possible to telex out. I have to go there with Kuon to meet customers, etc. Also a gold detecting machine has been installed at Tokyo Airport. Investigations are already in process by his people there about how it can be dealt with.

'The following means of entry are open to us: One, having gained utmost knowledge of the machine, and discovered if and how to combat, direct polar flights via Copenhagen and Anchorage. The alternatives, bearing in mind that the machine is in Tokyo only, are via Hong Kong to Okinawa, Fukuoka and Nagoya.'

Chapter 7/Stop and Go

Apart from the problems of an unfavourable market and telex transfers, I had spent a great deal of my first two weeks in Brussels dealing with a more threatening situation, in the form of Shirak. Within an hour of my arrival he was on the telephone, screaming first that his brother was double-crossing him, then that I was. Because of this, he had cancelled all the carriers' flights.

I was at my wit's end.

Sometime later, after all the flights had been rebooked, he cancelled them again.

'Why the bloody hell . . . ?'

'Well, Adam hasn't arrived, has he? We've heard nothing. He's been caught, hasn't he?'

'No he has not. We're not meant to have heard anything. No news is good news, remember. We'd have heard only if he'd been stopped.'

Each time that Shirak telephoned it was during a paranoic fit; and each time the cause for his fear turned out to be because he didn't understand what was going on; and usually this was because he had not read the procedure manuals.

He had also demanded that Paul be removed from the London Office and that if he wasn't he would end the business. Paul was undoubtedly our best man and I couldn't risk him being attacked by Shirak so I returned to London, assured Shirak that everything was all right, asked him to observe to the letter the procedures which had been agreed between us, then flew Paul back to Brussels. But in case Shirak issued any of his 'this is the end of the business' threats to Hong Kong, I wrote to Ben:

'I don't want to involve you in any complications this end because you have enough to deal with yourself. But it is important for you to know that our existence has been, and continues to be, seriously threatened by the uncontrollable lunatic and sudden rabid seizures of Shirak. He has gone through the motions of completely stopping this business several times, destroying and fucking up everyone and everything in sight. I'll spare you the details, but please don't think that I'm exaggerating.

'My own opinion, supported by his brother, who apart from his own axes to grind, has the survival of his organisation at heart, is that Shirak must be drawn out of the running of the business – or, frankly, we are quite soon going to be finished.

'I'm not suggesting that he ceases to be considered as a partner, indeed he must continue to be humoured as one. His percentage will be paid but he must be kept out of the way.

'I suggest meanwhile that you ignore any communication coming from him which tells you that this business is finished or to comply with any request which involves any departure from normal procedures or contradicts any instructions you receive from here. He has threatened to call you several times, which is why I write.'

During the third week carriers 'L8' and 'L9' and 'L10' were despatched. The load was reduced from fourteen to thirteen kilos. There were two reasons why it had not been reduced to twelve. First, we had been able to stall on the payment of carriers' tickets (at £450 a time) by paying by cheques, which were then met by seconds, as the proceeds of sales were speedily transferred from Hong Kong to Brussels and the necessary portion from there to London. Worthless cheques drawn on overdrawn accounts were floating around all over the place and hair-splitting timing was involved to ensure that no damage was done and that all were finally met. The second reason was that Kuon had made us a $2,500 interest-free loan.

The fourth week, we sent carriers to Singapore and

Bangkok instead of Hong Kong. But only the most trusted carriers were sent to Bangkok as they had to make the delivery themselves. On arrival the carrier had to take his load to a jewellers where he presented half of a dollar bill to the proprietor. The bill was matched· with the other half which Ben had sent to the shop. The carrier then deposited his load, returning two hours later to collect the payment which was in U.S. dollars. This he took to Hong Kong where it was telexed back to Brussels. In Singapore the carrier had to proceed to the Plantation Hotel where a room had been booked for him. As in Hong Kong he remained there until contacted, delivering to whoever called and introduced himself with the pre-arranged code name 'Ma Song'. In this case before the gold was delivered, payment had already been made in Hong Kong and transferred back to Brussels. Thereafter, we continued running into Hong Kong and made isolated deliveries in these two places. Another was made to Manila. But with prices in Bangkok, Manila and Singapore only two to five dollars above that of Hong Kong, and with insufficient customers to run regular routes into these places, we were still a long way from the prospected millions. The price situation in Hong Kong had to impiove. All we could do was wait, and while waiting prepare for an entry into Japan where the price was fifty-seven dollars an ounce and the total market was worth three million dollars a year to us. The prospect was encouraging but the routines would take months to set up by which time we might have no money left to finance the route. Fortunately we were presented with an alternative. The following letter was received from Ben:

'Here on holiday from Seoul is a leading representative of the Bank of America in Korea who I recently met at a dinner party. This is the information I have from him:

'The price in Korea is $82 an ounce – *double the world official price*. He will make introductions to possible clients whom he knows. He can arrange U.S. dollars in payment. It will not be possible to telex out, so they will have to be carried out. The officials at the airport, he assures me, are unbelievable. They are turning themselves inside out for tourists. All tourists get 15 per cent or 20 per cent off hotel bills, etc. I am spending Monday and Tuesday with him. He is going back at the end of the week and will send further information back by letter. Naturally his only personal involvement will be 'introducing', and he wants something out of it for himself. He doesn't think it's a huge market, but it doesn't have to be at that price. Even if the market ceiling were only fifteen pieces per month, I would be delirious.'

Two days later a carrier returned from Hong Kong with the following continuation.

'Since my last letter I have received more detailed information on Korea from my contact at Bank of America. His name, by the way, is Daniel Grant. He is British, was born in Hong Kong and educated in America. He is obviously very eager to make money and I can't imagine anyone more suitable to have as an initial contact in a proposed new market.

'There is a man called McQueen whose front is a machine tool importing company but who in reality is the big man in black market currency. Daniel's American wife, Phyllis, works for McQueen and is in his confidence, due particularly to Daniel's usefulness in the bank. The product in which we specialise has been known to have been mentioned frequently in her presence. He will be our main hope of changing Korean currency (wan) into dollars. Otherwise we may find them inconvertible.

'Calculations as follows:- The selling price, to repeat, is $82. Size of market unknown. Currency conversion normally results in a 20 per cent loss. However, Daniel suggests that, in view of the large sums involved, we will get a much more favourable rate of exchange. At this point I must stress that all information enclosed herein has to be investigated and affirmed by me first hand at source – i.e. with the people with whom we shall be dealing.

'As for communication from Korea, all overseas calls and cables are monitored. However, mail despatched through the A.P.O., the Military Post Office, is one hundred per cent safe – though it takes some time.

'Please advise me at speed on your decision regarding Korea. Do you wish me to go up? The cost of a return flight is $340. Bear in mind the fact that once there I will be unable to communicate and will therefore be able to send no reports until I am back in Hong Kong.'

I flew to London to discuss the matter with Shirak. While Ben was away – he might be gone for ten days – it would be necessary to suspend operations entirely.

Shirak approved enthusiastically. Even running only one load into Korea every ten days, while continuing with Hong Kong, and sending occasional loads into Bangkok, Singapore and Manila, would make us substantial profits. The behaviour of the Hong Kong market had now fallen into line with the European markets so we could afford to move into Japan leisurely, the prospects in Korea however drove this from our minds. I cabled Ben to go ahead.

It was six days later when I received a cablegram back, asking me to call at midnight, Central European Time. The same afternoon I went to the bank and purchased twenty-four kilos, hoping that Ben would have good news. If we did go into Korea then whoever took the gold in would be taking a big risk and he would have to know how big; I chose Paul Cotton.

'The chances are,' I said, 'that you will be requested to take the load on to Korea. Do you have any objection? We have no idea what the penalty is. For all I know it could be fifteen years.'

'They'll have to strip me to find out anything, won't they!' he said. He had been magnificently brainwashed!

I sent him to get a visa.

C

That evening I telephoned Ben.

'Korea is okay,' he said. 'But if we're going to run a regular route there, I think you should go there too. Conditions are a little tricky. First problem is not being able to keep a man there for more than fourteen days. Definitely not a place for sending in 'C's' [carriers] on blind dates.'

'Okay. I'll be out in about three days. By the way, Paul is actually on his way out. He'll be with you around six tomorrow. At the President.'

I gave Karbi his full instructions on the despatch of carriers to Hong Kong and flew to London. After a six hour search I found Shirak and asked him what he thought of my going to Korea. He approved. I obtained my visa.

A telegram arrived from Paul, at the London Office: 'ARRIVED STOP AM LONELY'. For reasons unknown Ben had failed to pick him up. Perhaps one of us had got the day wrong. But this was no cause for concern. Paul's instructions were to remain in his room until contacted.

I flew to Frankfurt, where I stayed the night, then caught a Pan Am flight for Hong Kong. There I spent four days, which were mostly taken up meeting Ben's contacts.

The flight to Seoul, the South Korean capital, via Thailand's Royal Orchid Service, was a luxurious experience. Escorted to our seats by hostesses in their brightly coloured saris, we were presented with icy damp perfumed towels to wipe the sweat from our brows and exquisite purple fans to whip up a cool breeze; brought cold jasmine tea, cherry wine, cocktails and exotic delicacies; and generally slaved upon in gracious and untiring service. Though I sat with Ben, as a precaution Paul sat apart from us and there was no communication between us. He was carrying. Further precautions had been taken in advance. Our visas had been obtained in Hong Kong, Brussels and London, while our disembarkation cards would show different hotels and ultimate destinations.

After some time we descended for a transit stop in Taiwan,

the Nationalist Republic of China. Here Ben had made some arrangements.

Large Hercules transport planes and camouflaged jets lined the runway; otherwise the airport was quite deserted. Disembarkation was compulsory, possibly a tourist trap, and we were warned not to take photographs. It was the height of summer. A hot steamy blast suffocated our nostrils and stuck to our bodies as we stepped into searing sunlight. Ben had assured me that his contact would be waiting and I was curious how he would bypass stringent security measures and get into the transit lounge.

We walked to the shopping centre. I wandered to a stall selling snakeskin belts, browsed for a while, finally bought one, then joined Ben who was at a stall selling toys close by.

'This is my partner,' he said, almost unexpectedly. The salesman looked at me quickly, then back at Ben. I left him to find the answers to his questions. How much gold could this man take himself? Could he find other customers for us and if so would he act as our agent? Would he arrange collection from our carriers? And how? Did he have any facilities for transferring money out of the country?

We returned to the plane. It was another four hours to Seoul. Ben's contact in Taiwan could guarantee disposal of up to fifty kilos a month immediately and beyond this he would let us know in a couple of months.

PART TWO

Chapter 8/Korea: A Proposition

'Daniel has a fantastic proposition,' Ben had said. 'I don't know all the details but it's to do with bank codes. They're worth a million dollars, two millions, more. He wants to do up his own bank, can you imagine?'

I could but wasn't particularly interested. I had had no doubt that Ben would come up with no end of propositions, once in the Far East; but I had told him emphatically, on the eve of his departure from London, that I didn't want to hear of any propositions unconnected with gold until we had at least three regular and major routes going. If we concentrated on doing this we would have our millions. The greatest danger was to be side-tracked. Even one trip a week with only twenty-four kilos was worth almost exactly one and a half million dollars net a year.

I was not pleased with Ben at this time. He had told me that he had one definite buyer in Korea and another possible. However, I had discovered in Hong Kong that despite his trip and original report we had no definite sale lined up – just a strong expectancy of one. This was not enough and the preparatory work he had done had been miserably inadequate. The consequence was that we were now going virtually blind into a country next on the danger list after Red China. The whole principle of our approach was wrong.

'But there's Daniel's proposition,' he kept saying. You've got to meet him. This man's worth his weight in gold. He'll give us anything we want. He'll throw the whole facilities of his bank at our disposal. When you hear the proposition you'll change your mind. Anyway, if you don't like it, there are others.'

Paul went through entry formalities ahead of us, then disappeared. We walked in single file through health and passport control. At passport control we were given a ticket with a number on it signifying which of the four customs, control points to go through. I went to the wrong one to see if the procedure was enforced. It was and I was redirected. Standing in the appropriate queue, I noticed Paul further off in the hall being questioned by two grim-faced men in baggy grey suits.

We entered the main entrance hall. Ben's friend Daniel was there to meet us. Paul, we hoped, would emerge shortly. His instructions were to ignore us totally and take a taxi to the Bondo Hotel. Should it be fully booked he was to try two other hotels in the city in the order I had given him. Should he have no luck with these he was to go ten miles out of the city to the Walker Hill Paradise Resort where he would certainly find a vacancy. In any case he was to move there the following morning. He was to remain in his room until contacted and throughout his stay in the country he would have no means of contacting us.

After Paul had finally emerged we left the airport. Ben went to a waiting car from which he could keep an eye on Paul's progress from a safe distance. Daniel drove me away in his army surplus jeep.

'What a relief!' he sighed, as we left the airport. 'They've just put a machine in, you know.'

'What!' I exclaimed.

He produced a paper from the locker. 'GOLD DETECTING MACHINE INSTALLED AT AIRPORT', was the inside page headlines. The paper, an American forces one, was dated the previous week.

'That's funny. How come they let our man through then?' I asked, realising as I spoke that they could have done so in order to follow him to his contacts.

'Didn't you get my telegram?' he asked.

'No,' I replied, lying. 'What telegram?'

'I sent one yesterday morning.'

'Perhaps it got delayed by your censors.'

'No. It was sent via the military.'

'What did it say?'

'Well, it told you not to come.'

'Really?' I feigned astonishment. 'Why?'

'It's impossible to do anything here at present. There are too many scares on. Fifteen people have been caught in the last month and now they've installed the machine.'

'What kind of people?'

'Koreans, Chinese, American servicemen. There was a large group of them, but several isolated cases as well.'

'How did they get caught?'

'Tip-offs, all of them. Once a Korean gets hold of one they catch the lot – always. It's no holds barred. They start to pull his fingernails out. He talks! He knows they mean business. They're cruel bastards – worse than the Japanese.'

We were driving through the outskirts of the city – a mass of shacks. The streets were teeming with people.

'You can't do business with the Koreans: you're slitting your own throat as soon as you open your mouth. They've an estimated four hundred thousand paid informers of the C.I.A., all busy with ears, eyes and feelers everywhere, gleaning information and trading it as a means of livelihood as well as a sport. Three thousand pounds is offered as a tip which might lead to the capture or death of an infiltrator or agent. They don't ask questions either. If a finger is pointed they shoot. They're worse than Macarthyites.'

I listened intently, murmuring polite astonishments.

'A small column of soldiers was marching towards Seoul a few weeks ago, quite openly. Somebody claimed they were communists disguised in South Korean uniform so they were ambushed, machine-gunned, and there was not one surviver.

'A drunken taxi driver was driving home last week after curfew. He was ordered to halt, obviously didn't hear, drove on, and was immediately shot.'

'Delightful place! I wouldn't have thought it was one for any Chinaman to come to.'

'Well, there are quite a few of them here.'

'What about the Chinese who got caught? Were they Korean based?'

'I don't know. They caught one, thinking he was a North Korean agent.'

'Yes?'

'Yes. Now I come to think of it, he wasn't Korean based. He had arrived off the plane and wasn't met by his contact. Couldn't find a hotel. Everywhere was booked up. The accommodation situation is dreadful. He couldn't walk about the streets at night carrying thirty to forty kilos, so he slept in some back yard. In the morning he grabbed a taxi. You can imagine how dishevelled he looked. The driver thought "Ah! I've got an agent," and whisked him straight off to the police station.'

'Poor chap. What are the penalties?'

'It's difficult to say. Anything from five to fifteen years. It seems to vary according to the mood.'

The city was barely less a dump than the suburbs and looked as if it was still under siege. Soldiers and armed police were everywhere. The roads, even the main ones in the centre, were dirt-tracks, and many of them had been torn to shreds by tanks. Three-quarters of the entire population of men seemed to be carrying or pulling something, either on bare backs or on scaffolding-type structures strapped to their bodies or on bicycles piled so high that they were unable to see either around or over the tops of their loads so young kids had to run in front as pilots. And in contrast to the chic, radiant faces of the girls in Hong Kong there were only ugly, plump, sullen ones here.

'The place sounds like a pretty good hell-hole,' I said to Daniel.

'I can't get out quick enough.'

'Why is it impossible to do anything here?'

'It's impossible now and will be for the next few months. Once the Koreans get hold of something they don't stop chewing it. They chew it with a fanaticism until it's twice dead then they forget it and chew something else. It's too dangerous at the moment and I can tell you with absolute certainty that you must not talk with any Korean direct – whether he is a government official or not.'

What Daniel was saying was a dramatic reversal of the impressions he had given Ben. In fact he seemed to be saying 'I'm afraid I've been carried away in my enthusiasm and the fact is that I now realise that I won't be able to find customers. In fact I am most hesitatingly and regretfully obliged to be of any assistance to you at all. I am also shit scared.'

'Didn't Ben realise the situation when he was up here?' I asked – meaning, 'Surely you told him what you have just told me?'

'The situation wasn't so acute then,' he said.

'The machine report could be a bluff.' I suggested. 'At any rate it can't have been installed yet. Issuing a report that one has been installed is just as effective as actually having one. Anyway, within a few weeks, there's a good chance that we'll have a remedy against it. I'm waiting for a reply from a scientific laboratory in the States to find out whether there is any substance or material that can block the penetration of the low energy gamma rays emitted by the radio isotope – as, for example, carbon paper blocks X-rays. Then perhaps we can either coat the gold or re-line our suits with something.'

'It would be typical of the Koreans if they only used it on people going out!' he said.

'Really?'

'Really. There's no telling.'

We were still driving past rows of filthy huts, being jolted violently by the pot-holed surface of the road. Suddenly we took a sharp turn left into a narrow lane, weaved our way a couple of hundred yards down it, avoiding boulders and gashes almost deep enough to be classified as trenches, and came to a field. There was a small moat, a bank, a pit and another bank between us and the field, but the ground was reasonably dry and the jeep just managed to scramble over them.

We finally came to a halt in front of an iron gateway which was supported on each side by high concrete walls topped with broken glass. Daniel pressed the bell and shortly a giggling peasant women in her middle thirties came out to greet us. We drove through the grounds to a pleasant modern bungalow. I took off my shoes and left them on the patio before going in. Daniel mixed drinks and we waited for Ben and Phyllis, Daniel's wife.

They appeared an hour later.

'Where is it?' I asked Ben.

'It's under the back seat of the car.'

'Fine. By the way, who were the men at the airport?'

'I don't know. I've had no further contact with Paul.'

We didn't talk about business until after dinner when we talked of nothing else. I was going to pump Daniel for everything useful he knew.

'What's the price situation?' I asked.

'The last figure published was eighty-two dollars an ounce.'

'Published by whom?'

'The main American Forces Paper.'

'How is the price established?'

'It's fixed by the Government. It's the price at which they sell to jewellers. There's no market as such. Every now and again – maybe once a month – the Government decides to sell. By the way, it isn't European gold. It's the local Chinese type orange gold which they prefer and use almost exclusively.'

'What?' I exclaimed in disbelief. Someone had bungled.

'But it's inferior stuff,' I told him. 'Is nobody interested in what we have? Whoever else is operating into this country must have a market. Who buys it?'

'At some point or other it has to be blended I suppose.'

'Any idea what the pre-blended black market price is?'

'None. McQueen would know.'

'He'd know all right, but it would hardly be in his interest to make a confession of it. Have you seen him recently?'

'Yes, he came to see me this morning. I mentioned the subject to him and he's definitely not interested.'

Another hope struck off!

'I'll go and sound out the scene of the jewellers in the morning,' said Ben.

I scowled at him. Ben would have to do a lot more than that to make up for getting us involved in this scene.

'I've told you already', said Phyllis, 'that you must not contact or have any dealings with Koreans.'

'They're totally unscrupulous and dishonest,' explained Daniel. 'The hobby of every single one of them is doing up any other single one of them. They'll do it for money or just out of habit. They're treacherous. Where they have failed they can't bear another to succeed. Success therefore is short lived. When one of them succeeds, two or three of his friends will then get together and plan his destruction, using any form of maliciousness or lying.'

'You mean it's fish eats fish.'

'Yes, they're the only people in the world whom you can rely on to kill the goose that lays the golden eggs every time. They have no religion or culture and have created nothing. They're barbarous and without scruple.'

'How does McQueen manage?' I asked.

'Well, he's survived fifteen years or so one must assume that he's extremely crafty. He also has a beautiful and bright young Korean wife.'

'That'll be something to see, a beautiful Korean.'

'You'll see her. She's at the Seoul swimming pool every day.'

'Have you told Roderic your proposition?' Ben asked, abruptly changing the subject. This was the moment he had been waiting for, the moment when Daniel would finally drop his formal front and disclose his scheme to me. 'Honestly, I can't keep my eyes open a second longer,' continued Ben. 'I'm flaked out.'

'Let's move from the table.'

'I'm going to bed,' declared Ben.

'You're joking. We're only just starting!' I said.

'No, I'm dead.'

'Come on. You can't let the side down.'

'I'm ill,' he said with some emphasis.

'Doesn't matter,' I replied.

He glared at me furiously and fiercely. A few minutes later he was asleep on the couch.

'It's very simple,' Daniel opened up. 'Do you know anything about telex?'

'Only that we use it to transfer the proceeds of our sales back to Europe.'

'You know nothing about the internal procedures involved?'

'Nothing.'

'Well, money which has to be transferred urgently is sent either by cable or telex. In both, a code is used. If you have the code you can send as much money as you like and the receiving bank is bound to pay out. It's almost as simple as that.'

'Really? Fantastic! Have you ever sent one?'

'I'm sending them all the time.'

'By telex or cable?'

'I've used both but we have no cable link with the outside world here so I have to go to the Post Office and send a cable from there.'

'Naturally you have the code numbers?' I said.

'We have access to whatever we want.'

'In what form does the cable arrive at the bank?' I thought

it best to go once through the main details so that I could have the next day to chew on them.

'Exactly as you send it.'

'It arrives as an ordinary telegram through the post box with letters in the morning or by special delivery?'

'Exactly.'

'There would be nothing suspicious in the fact that an instruction to pay out a large sum arrived in this way and not directly on the telex machine?'

'Nothing. So long as the code and the styling of the instruction are correct, nothing else matters. There can be many reasons why instructions arrive by cable and not by telex. A bank may have no telex, or it may have one without having any direct link with the receiving bank, or its machine could be temporarily out of order or the operator ill.'

'Here. I'll show you exactly what one looks like.' He reached in his pocket. 'I received this a couple of weeks back from the Hang Seng Bank in Hong Kong instructing me to pay out $60,000 to the Pourougehang Trading Company in Seoul. You see it's just an ordinary cable. The "L.T." means "Letter Rate" which shows it was sent from a Post Office or by phone to a Post Office.'

'By phone?'

'Yes the Bank quotes its cable code name which in this case happens to be "Habindo", as you see, by which it has signed itself. We have a book of code names and numbers of banks all over the world. These are kept by the manager himself, though sometimes by one other senior official. They are kept only at National Head Offices, never at Branch offices. They are a bank's most carefully guarded possession.'

'Have the codes ever been broken?'

'No.'

'How do you know?'

'I worked for six years in the cable department of our Head Office in San Francisco so I would have learnt if they had. In any case the codes would have been changed if they'd been broken – and they never have been.'

He pointed to the cable. 'The message is always preceded by the numerical code – in this case, 791. This is not just one code, but the sum of several others. There's a code for the transmitting bank, depending on which bank it is and in which city in which country, and there's a similar code for the receiving bank. There's also one for the kind of currency which is being transmitted, the day of the week, one for the month, one for the date and several for the sum of money – one for the tens, one for the hundreds, one for the thousands, one for the ten thousands. These are all added up, and the final figure is that used on the message.'

'Very clever.'

'Now I'll show you exactly how this one is made up,' he said, pulling some sheets of pencilled figures out of his pocket. 'I have here all the codes relevant to this particular cable. You call out the details of the message, I'll call out the relevant numbers which you can take down. Add them up and you'll be able to check that the figure of 791 on this cable is correct.'

It was. We reversed the process using his extracts from the bank code and I called out the numbers to him.

He had explained the codes; now he explained the phrasing which was as follows:

'791 REIMBURSE YOURSELVES BANK OF AMERICA SAN FRANCISCO. PAY 60,000 DOLLARS POUROUGEHANG TRADING COMPANY ORDER SOUTH CHINA TRADING COMPANY. HABINDO'

'We are instructed to pay $60,000 to the Pourougehang Trading Company by "Habindo" – the cable code name for the Hang Seng Bank in Hong Kong. At the same time, we must be reimbursed by them. Now they don't have an account with us in Korea but they have one with our Head Office in San Francisco. What happens is that we notify San Francisco that we've received the cable. They process the details in their books by crediting our account with them and debiting the account of the Hang Seng Bank, issuing them with a debit note. The Hang Seng will receive this note no earlier than ten days after they have sent their original cable instruction to us which means that we will have *ten clear days* after collection of the money before they discover that the cable was a fraud.'

'What checks does the receiving bank make on the authenticity of the cable?'

'There are standard procedures to be followed. Here.' He gave me a dozen pages of photostated regulations. 'You can go through them tomorrow. The number code is always double checked. The cable word-code should also be checked, but generally isn't. The correct styling of a message will be recognised immediately.'

'If the manager of the receiving bank was in any doubt, what would or could he do about it?'

'The most likely cause of doubt would have nothing to do with the authenticity of the cable. What the manager would question was whether the instructing bank had sufficient credit balances with his Head Office or not. If in doubt he would cable Head Office. He would do so automatically if it was a small bank or there wasn't much correspondence between them.'

'Whatever banks we chose,' he added, 'I will know if the instructing bank has sufficient balances with the Head Office of the receiving one and also that there are frequent transactions between them. The Hang Seng, I know, have credit balances at our Head Office running into tens of millions.'

'Are you sure?'

'Perfectly.'

'What if the bank code were wrong?'

'Well, fraud would be suspected immediately. The manager would make an on-the-spot check with the instructing bank, either by telex or telephone.'

'In that case, we have to choose banks which have no

direct telex link and days when it's impossible to make a telephone check. Do you have a list of bank holidays in different countries?'

'Yes.'

'Then we'll chose our day according to that.'

'Fine, but I assure you that if the phrasing and numerical code are correct the cable won't be doubted for a moment.'

'What makes you so certain?'

'Because I have frequently paid out myself, because I have seen payouts of very large amounts, because twenty-five years of successful usage of the coding system has conditioned habits in the minds of those concerned with an automatic assumption that a cable, properly phrased and coded, must be correct. In addition, it's too improbable that a man chosen to be Head Office manager or his assistant will ever be involved in any such fraud attempt.'

'It's a fantastic proposition, Daniel. I'll take these photostats with me and we can talk some more tomorrow. How much were you thinking of doing it for?'

'Two to three million dollars,' he said.

'That's too much.'

'Well, why not?'

'Perhaps, we can talk about the exact sum later.'

He nodded. I left. Ben had sold him hard on the organisation, that was obvious. Daniel imagined us to be a superbly efficient machine and one good enough to handle an operation which had obviously been on his mind for a long time, while in him we had found every crook's dream – a bent bank official.

Chapter 9/Korea: Around Seoul

Early next day Daniel and his wife drove into Seoul, leaving Ben and me to discuss him and his proposition. We agreed on most points. Daniel was weak, had little guts, and was easily influenced – particularly by his domineering wife. Suffering their isolation, they welcomed our company with open arms. They were frustrated, anxious about the future, and desperate to escape from Korea. They viewed us as possible saviours. The proposition was workable – and irresistible. It was original. We decided to go through the motions of accepting it. We might need it.

Daniel had made it plain that he wasn't going to help us with the gold so we would have to work on our own. There were two possibilities: Bedian, an old acquaintance of Ben's, and McQueen.

Ben telephoned Bedian but there was no reply. McQueen could only be found at the Seoul Club, a meeting place for Europeans and their wives, as he had requested not to be contacted at his home or office. He was generally at the club around lunchtime. Ben left to spend the day there if necessary. After half an hour of lounging in the sun I returned to my papers. I studied Daniel's photostat copies of his bank's internal procedures on telex transfers, digested them completely, browsed through Korean trade journals, and did accounts.

Before finishing the day, I filed the following information on Daniel Grant – under the name 'Judith Elroy' and abbreviated: 'Aged thirty, earns $1,000 a month all expenses paid, saves everything. Anxious to invest $10,000 in gold or telex. He will get interest at the rate of $100 a trip into Hong Kong, payable when we want to pay. Loan for period unspecified. His intention: to come in with us full time. He will invest the bulk of his share of the telex operation in our businesses. Has tremendous amount of information to offer. Completely committed.'

Ben returned with our hosts early in the evening.

McQueen hadn't appeared and Bedian's number had remained unanswered.

We spent the remainder of the day talking about the telex proposition.

We discussed partnership terms. Daniel suggested a fifty-fifty split which I thought to be unreasonable, considering that he would be doing none of the work. After arguing for some time we left the matter open.

The next day I accompanied Ben and Daniel into the city. A dreadful sickly smell hung in the air. The outward conditions of the people, many crippled as a result of the war, toiling under excessive burdens and living in the filthiest squalor, were pitiful. Gnarled, resigned faces spoke out words I remembered – Van Gogh, Sartre, Dostoevsky: 'Misery will never end' – 'We are trapped in physical filth and there is no way out,' – 'Existence is absurd, yet I live.' To survive, was it any wonder that dog ate dog? 'There is no hope for us but we dare to believe that there is hope for our children.' Children were everywhere. Out-of-work teenagers lounged in jeans and peaked caps on every street corner.

We were dropped at the Bondo Hotel, and entered. Groups of Koreans in dark suits, with short back and sides and severe arrogant expressions were scattered everywhere. They occupied the lounge, the bar, the breakfast room, read the papers or just stood; and they were there in the hallway, in little changed positions, an hour later, when we came out. Sinister.

We lunched at the Seoul Club, joined by Daniel who had brought more information for me to study, and lounged in the sun all afternoon, waiting for McQueen who didn't show, while watching his exceedingly delectable lush-figured wife spittooning herself in the briefest of bikini pants and a precariously perched unleashed bra. Ben had called Bedian to learn that he was due back from Tokyo the following morning. Events could not be made to happen. There was little to do but wait.

On our fourth day, Ben lunched with Bedian – alone. Bedian was exceptionally suspicious and cautious, so Ben would have to re-establish his earlier rapport before I was introduced. Besides being our sole contact in Korea Bedian had formerly been one of the largest distributors of black market gold in Japan and would be able to give us valuable introductions there.

Ben returned in the evening with far from encouraging results. Bedian already had sufficient stock which he would not or could not dispose of. Also he had been reliably informed that a machine had been installed at the airport; and nothing he said contradicted what we had already heard. He would help us in any way he could but extended very little hope This was discouraging but it had to be remembered that if Bedian was interested in buying then it would be in his interest to paint the picture black.

After lunch, Ben had returned to the Club and met McQueen. No, McQueen said, he was definitely not interested in our commodity. However, he would be able to change whatever wan we had, though he wouldn't quote a price until we were in a position to do business. What he couldn't change in Korea, subject to three or four days' notice, he would change in Hong Kong – no doubt at our expenses. An hour later he had approached Ben: 'On that other matter, I will make what enquiries I can.'

At dinner that evening we discussed our new project in greater detail. Daniel had returned with more material from the bank, including a list of bank holidays in every country in the world so we could find the best dates for transferring between one bank and another, and eliminate a whole area of risk.

Daniel insisted that his bank, the Bank of America, should

not be the one to lose money. He gave his reason as a feeling of loyalty to them which struck me as being ridiculous, although I had no practical reason for objecting. Branches of his bank in other countries would be the most suitable to collect from, as he knew all the internal procedures of transfer and pay-out and could easily find out the credit balances which his bank held at its head office in San Francisco in favour of the Hang Seng Bank in Hong Kong – whose name, cable and numerical codes we had decided to use.

We decided to collect in Europe, and considered Zurich, Amsterdam, Brussels, Antwerp, Geneva and London. This list was eventually shortened to Zurich and Amsterdam, two active business centres, one with a large gold market, and the other a large diamond market, where large cash withdrawals are a regular occurrence.

We discussed the sizes of sums to be transferred and finally agreed on $600,000.

The ideal dates were the 2nd and 5th of August, conveniently on either side of the week-end, with the 5th being a bank holiday in Hong Kong.

Daniel would not be involved in the execution of the plan. He would not leave Korea until at least six months after the event. I would send somebody from England to send the cables as Ben was too well known in the colony.

Prior to the final cable, several legitimate transfers of money would be sent to our two collectors in Zurich and Amsterdam in order to build their confidences as well as those of the managers of the banks. Such sums of money would be sent back to Hong Kong, via yet another bank and fed back into the pipeline. It was thought that if the bank managers doubted the first instruction to pay out and checked it by telephone then subsequently they would relax. Also the collector would get to know the routine and become familiar with the kind of delays which might otherwise disturb him on the vital day.

'What about the collector's "front" and approach?' I asked Daniel.

'Well, the sooner he strikes up a personal relationship with the manager, maybe even taking him out to lunch, the better.'

'That's too dangerous. Our men won't be able to put themselves across as businessmen in such close contact. Supposing the man in Zurich declared himself as a gold smuggler?' I asked. 'Would this be a matter of concern to the managers?'

'Not at all. They would be delighted with the business.'

'I thought so, judging from the response of our bank managers. Also such a declaration offers a very plausible explanation for drawing out large sums in cash.'

'Quite.'

'Also this would fit in very well with an "after the event" disposal solution. Traceable cash could be converted instantly into untraceable goods. Both diamonds and gold may be purchased anonymously. Perhaps the man in Amsterdam could ask for letters of introduction to reputable dealers there, ask his manager to advise him on finding offices and so forth, and establish his "front" in this way.'

'Why not?'

'On the other hand,' I continued, 'this might result in leaving behind some very obvious traces. The bank's investigators would deduce that the people who pulled off the coup were smugglers because of the obvious connection between Zurich and Hong Kong.'

We left this problem to be discussed later.

'What traces will the collectors be leaving, anyway?' I wondered aloud.

'That's your department,' Daniel replied.

'I know, but we may as well discuss it. They will enter the country, stay in hotels and leave the country. They can't use their own names so we'll have to get false passports. That's a problem. They're easy to obtain but it would mean contacting the London hoodery and it's a small world, so we would lay ourselves open to blackmail. All in all, buying them on the market would be a bad security risk.'

'Why not get them in Hong Kong?' Daniel suggested.

'Too many additional complications,' I said.

'Maybe I can arrange for the boys to get British Visitors Passports.'

'What about a passport for my assistant?' Ben asked.

'He doesn't really need one,' I replied. 'It's not necessary for him to open a bank account. He can arrive at the Hang Seng Bank, plonk the cash on the counter and transmit it under any name. They have the money and his real identity is of no concern to them.'

'What bank can we use for sending the money back to Hong Kong?' I asked. 'The First National City? Does it have branches in Zurich and Amsterdam?'

'I'll check.' replied Daniel.

'Who can the money be sent back to?'

'It can be sent straight to my account,' suggested Ben.

'That I don't like.'

'Why not? It's perfectly legit.'

'Yes, but it's an unnecessary link. Can't you think of anybody else? The possibility of an initial two-way flow of money could be guessed, and records of all telex transfers between Amsterdam, Zurich and Hong Kong during the period prior to the event might be checked.'

This was the second problem to be left temporarily aside.

We agreed that there would be no further contact between ourselves and Daniel once we had left Korea. Somehow, however, he would have to be informed of the success of the venture. This would be done anonymously. I would instruct a European bank to donate the sum of one hundred dollars to a Korean charity which banked at the Bank of America in Seoul. He would note the sum arriving via telex machine and know that everything was okay. Once we had left Korea, it would be impossible to change the plan – because the codes were tied to specific amounts and dates.

Daniel's only concern was with the collection. The problem of conversion, subsequent transfer and safe-keeping of the proceeds was to be left to me and he didn't doubt that we would look after his interest.

'You don't need to worry about the notes being traceable,' he said suddenly, returning to my proposal to purchase diamonds and gold. 'No record will be kept of them.'

'We can't take a chance on that,' I said, 'and it won't hurt to assume that a record will be kept. Also if we don't convert into diamonds and gold we'll have to change the money into small bills over the counters of lots of different banks.'

'Why can't the money be telexed straight out?' Ben suggested.

'It could be traced,' Daniel told him.

'Or we could bury the lot in safe deposit boxes,' Ben offered. 'We can change it up months later.'

'We have ten clear days in which to solve the problem,' Daniel reminded him, 'let's solve it within that time. Purchase gold and place that in safety boxes – that is a possibility?'

'Where will the heat come from?' I asked. 'Who will be involved in subsequent investigations and what steps will they take? First of all, who actually stands to suffer the financial loss?'

'The Hang Seng,' he replied. 'But each bank will be accusing the other of a leakage in one of their branches. The whole event is going to be extremely embarrassing for both of them because the only deduction to be drawn is that a very high official in one of their banks is involved. It's my opinion that the police will not be called, but that investigations will be handled exclusively by the banks' own investigators, who are more thorough and tenacious than any police, I assure you. They will be terrified of any publicity, and they will avoid it at all costs.

'There is an unwritten law, understood between banks, concerning the liability for payments and reimbursement for payments on forged documents. If any bank pays out on a document which could reasonably have been seen to be false, then that bank must suffer the consequences of its negligence. Each bank has specimens of current authorising signatures of other banks with which it is dealing, as well as samples of their forms of instructions; so, they have every facility for the required verifications. The unwritten law further implies that if the document is prima facie correct – even though it is subsequently proved to have been a forgery – then the bank whose authorisation has been forged is bound to honour it. In our case, the Hang Seng. If these principles were not upheld, then many features of the banking system would collapse. For example, if there was any doubt that the Hang Seng Bank would not honour documents in their name which were prima facie correct then other banks around the world would cease to have any confidence in paying out on them. In the banking world, confidence is everything.'

'The Hang Seng', he continued, 'will be obliged to honour the principle, because it will be both a matter of saving face as well as ultimately expedient.'

Knowing nothing of banking procedures at this level, I accepted his arguments, which seemed to make sense. But it was difficult to believe that a fraud of this size would be hushed up or the police left out of it. I imagined that there would be a shudder right through both banking organisations, followed by a swift realisation that whoever had the codes could strike again.

'A hue and cry', Daniel insisted, 'is exactly what both banks will avoid because it would make them both look ridiculous. They can't allow confidence in themselves to be publicly undermined and they won't call in the police because they'll consider their own investigators better equipped to deal with the matter and more likely to go on chewing the bone until they come to the marrow of it.'

'And will they ever finally throw it away?' I asked.

'I doubt it.' Daniel gave several accounts of their own bank investigators' methods and achievements in tracking culprits down.

'Every head office branch of the Bank of America in the world will become the object of their scrutiny. No expense or effort will be spared. They're coming here in a couple of weeks for a routine check.'

'That's good,' I said.

'Very convenient.'

'You'll have to stay on here as long as possible afterwards,' I said. 'They'll be looking for personnel changes. What explanation will you give for going anyway?'

'My wife couldn't take Korea,' he replied. 'I can arrange for her to see a doctor and obtain a certificate. She can start undergoing psychiatric treatment – as a result of which it will be recommended that her anxieties and neuroses can only increase so long as she remains here.'

'Okay, but they'll wonder why you didn't simply apply for a transfer to another branch? You'll have to tell them you're going to another bank or into a new field.'

'Even if they knew that I had been involved, they wouldn't be able to prove anything,' he said.

'Possibly. But to suspect might be good enough. They'd have you watched from that point on. They'd examine in detail what you're doing and with whom you have been associating over the past few months. They'd discover that one month ago you were on holiday with your wife in Hong Kong, and, most likely, whom you met there. Then they'd discover that you had English visitors.'

'Nobody knows that you've been staying here.'

'Your maid?'

'I'll sack her.'

'What about the Seoul Club? No,' I went on, 'We'll get rid of all cause for suspicion or avoid it right from the beginning. You'll have to stay here for at least twelve months. When you leave, it should be to move to a job with a much larger salary. Subsequently, we can find something for you.'

Our discussions continued into the early hours of the morning.

Chapter 10/Korea: The Crunch

It was twenty miles and sixteen road blocks to Walker Hill and the military badge on the front windscreen did not entitle us to pass unmolested.

As soon as we arrived I went to see Paul.

He explained that the men who had approached him at the airport had been journalists who had been told that he had 'actor' on his passport and had been interested in him as a possible celebrity.

I decided not to create any anxiety by telling him that there was a machine at the airport and that with our luck being as it was he might have to carry the gold back out. He was already a bit touchy. 'One has the feeling of being watched the whole time,' he said. 'And one is,' he added.

However, he was enjoying his life. He had been flabbergasted by the promptness with which the gold had been collected. 'Within thirty seconds after I had arrived in my room,' he said. 'And by a woman. She was incredibly beautiful. I really thought I was taking part in some film. The experience just didn't seem real. She just stood there as I undressed and handed the bars to her.'

Kept in total ignorance of our contacts he never discovered that this was Daniel's wife.

I told him that we would be in the country a further week and suggested that he stay on at Walker Hill, then I joined the others who were in the casino.

At nine the next morning we presented ourselves at KOTRA, the Korean Trade Organisation, to keep an appointment which had been arranged for us with the president of a wig manufacturing company. It was important that we considered our 'cover'. If we wished to return to Korea we would have genuine business reasons for doing so and have no difficulty in obtaining visas for repeated entries.

We returned to the Seoul Club. We had been at the pool an hour or so when McQueen waddled on to the scene – in bathing pants. He nodded to us discreetly and sat down by his wife. Not until another hour had passed did he approach us.

'Do you still have possession?' he asked.

The question was reassuring because it implied we had other contacts in the country. An important factor when it came to bargaining.

'I'll be in Japan for the next few days. Will you be here on my return?'

'Yes,' replied Ben. 'We have several interests to attend to.'

He remained standing during an exchange of little more than a minute so that our acquaintanceship would appear to be no more than a passing one.

In the early evening, we went to the British Embassy for a garden party in celebration of the Queen's birthday.

It was a quaint, punctiliously conducted affair, yet at the same time pleasantly informal. We met, amongst other people, the commercial attaché and his wife, to whom we were careful to put across our official fronts. We were importers and exporters representing the Parkstone Trading Company of Hong Kong. It was impossible not to wonder what they would have thought had they realised how helpful and charming they were being to a pair of smugglers.

The following day Ben and I were at the Bondo Hotel where we had arranged to meet Bedian at 11.30. He was half an hour late. When Ben spotted him we followed him through the lounge and outside where we were bundled into the back of a dusty van which drove out of Seoul and headed south. Conversation was minimal and guarded. He was about sixty and spoke with a strong mid-European accent. We arrived at his house and were introduced to his wife. He led us through to the lounge where he poured some drinks.

'Too much?' he queried, when the tumbler was almost full of neat Bourbon.

It was soon clear that Ben had done yet another of his magnificent sales jobs. Bedian had a very high opinion of us indeed.

We had been talking for some time when he mumbled something in a foreign tongue to his wife who promptly disappeared into the bedroom and returned with a black briefcase. From this he extracted files, letters and documents, and handed them to me. It didn't take long to see that they were contracts worth hundreds of thousands of dollars. The punch line was that he required finance in the form of letters of credit to import machinery from Japan. No Korean bank would provide the sum and he was having difficulties elsewhere. Would we do it? Yes we would, I said, in approximately three months time. He accepted my promise and I decided that it was time we talked about our gold. I asked him if he was interested in buying. Instead of answering he motioned us into his office, where he unlocked a safe to reveal rows of ten tola gold bars.

'I don't need to buy,' he said. 'Dealing is no longer my business.'

I didn't know whether I was more surprised by the gold or the trust he put in us. He shut the safe then led us back to the lounge.

We had lunch.

'After the hunters have ceased their current obsession with running operators into the ground, we can do good business here,' he said, 'but Koreans are not interested in fine yellow gold. For them it is not beautiful; nor does it have the magic of Chinese gold. There is only one way to sell European gold and that is by blending it. But to do this one must have the facilities. One needs to buy here also.'

'Buy here?' I asked, surprised.

'Yes. You can do so with a government licence. Now, listen to me. I have a plan.

'It is permitted to import under licence,' he continued, 'providing you are a maker of jewellery and provided the finished product is exported. See the possibility?'

I shook my head. He continued.

'This is precisely what you do. Start by producing invoices of purchase which can be checked and balanced against other evidence which shows that the same quantity of gold has been sent out. But who is to prove exactly what quantity of gold is in the jewellery that has been sent out?'

I saw exactly what he was suggesting.

'Naturally one starts off with a full quota. After that, one reduces the amount so that the jewellery is only gold-plated. The balance is siphoned out.'

'And melted into bars, having been blended with local gold,' I added.

'Which is then sold on the black market. Nobody is being cheated, because the company buying the jewellery from us, in Hong Kong, or in Europe, will be your company.'

'Brilliant,' I said.

'This is no longer smuggling. You understand? You will be able to dispense with carriers and there will be no machine problem. You will be able to purchase gold in Europe and ship or fly it in quite legally.'

'Do you have the facilities?' I asked.

'Yes I do. I will show them to you.'

His factory was a good thirty miles south. The main structure of it was complete but builders were everywhere. Half a dozen workers were turning out electrical components on machines. Bedian with several immediate problems to attend to, left us to stroll around. It was almost three hours later when he rejoined us. The last worker had left so he showed us where and how he did his blending. I pressed him once again about our load of gold. He was short of liquid cash, but thought he would raise a loan.

Being a Sunday, the banks were closed. We decided that we could spend a useful day uninterruptedly installed on the premises of the Bank of America – to which Daniel had a key.

We already had the codes for the telex plan, along with copies of the bank's internal procedures on the payout and processing of transfers; now we could obtain specimen signatures of bank managers and chief cashiers of every major bank in every city around the world, originals of all Bank of America documents, and any other valuable material we wished. We wished for a great deal, the opportunity being too good to miss.

On the premises there was a photocopying machine.

The situation seemed most unreal. Our presence, as intruders in the bank, was a relaxed one in which we could speak normally, brew coffee, browse or sit around as we chose, whereas intruders in other circumstances would be expected to be creeping stealthily around the place, gripped by nervous tension or fear, and communicating – if at all – in whispers. Ben the comedian came into his own.

We left – the safe intact. We had no interest in a few pilfered grand. The material we had, with the technical advice of a key bank man dedicated to our joint interests and totally at our service, was worth tens of millions.

Despite attractive visions, our immediate situation was still desperate. Five days later we had not heard from Bedian. We would soon have to leave Korea. To do so with no sale would be disastrous.

If he was playing a waiting game, hoping that we might come to him with a ridiculous offer, then the game had to be brought to a head. We decided not to approach him with an offer, but simply to inform him that we were leaving. McQueen had not returned from Japan, but we had little hope in him.

'I'm ringing up to say goodbye,' Ben said to Bedian on the telephone. 'We're leaving at crack of dawn tomorrow.'

D

'Oh! Have you sold?' he asked.

'No. We haven't but we have other business to attend to, which can't wait.'

'Surely you won't be taking the gold with you?'

'Yes.'

'But that's lunacy.'

'It's all right. We've arranged a safe exit.'

'I may have an interest in twelve,' he said. 'What price will you let me have them for?'

'As quoted,' Ben replied.

'Nothing off?'

'Nothing. It already represents a drop of twenty-five per cent.'

'I'll try to raise the money from the bank this morning.'

'Where do we do the transaction?' Ben asked me, covering the mouthpiece with his hand.

'Here,' I suggested. 'I'd feel much happier.'

'Good,' he said to Bedian. 'Would you like to come here for a drink around seven?'

He would. We were jubilant. Ben went into the city immediately to book a flight back to Hong Kong while I telephoned Paul, casually mentioning that I would be on the afternoon flight to Tokyo the next day – all calls being monitored – and wondering if by any chance he would be on the same flight. He didn't know yet, he said, knowing that he had no alternative.

In preparation for Bedian's visit I checked the gold, then thought about how the proceedings should be conducted. Daniel's house was beautifully situated for a handover, having an excellent command of all approaches. The exchange would take place in the bedroom, I decided. I positioned two bugs, set up a miniature automatic radio recorder, then considered the final problem. What was to be done with the remaining pieces? It would be ridiculous to risk the machine. The only answer seemed to be to bury them.

Bedian arrived an hour and a half late. He was carrying a bulky bag and several bundles. We took him straight to the bedroom.

'What have you got there?' Ben asked.

'Money,' said Bedian.

Ben gave an incredulous gasp.

'That's impossible,' he said.

'No it isn't. I have some more in the car. I must bring it in.'

'You have to be joking,' Ben insisted.

Bedian left and returned a few moments later with some more parcels.

'It was a squeeze getting it,' he explained. 'Anyway, I did the best I could. Afraid that I could only get a small quantity of 500 wan notes. The rest is in 100s.'

'So we see.'

I produced the bars.

'London?' he asked.

'Yes. 999 and all Johnson and Matthey.'

He began undoing his parcels.

'What the hell are we going to do with all this?' Ben asked. 'How the hell are we going to get it out?'

'I'll take twelve,' Bedian said, ignoring him.

'That's $23,040,' I replied, consulting my calculations. 'Or 6,220,800 wan.'

We counted the bundles. Some of them had disintegrated so the contents had to be re-sorted and counted. The job took twenty minutes. There were fifty bundles altogether.

'You have the others?' he asked.

'Yes.'

'Would it be possible for me to take them now and settle on credit?' he enquired. 'I can pay within the month.' he assured me, 'anywhere you like.'

'Hong Kong,' I said.

'Good. Give me the address of your bank. I'll have the money transferred from New York. I can't arrange this from here; but I can do so from Tokyo. I'm going there in the morning, Okay?' I looked at Ben. He nodded. 'Okay.'

'You trust me?' he asked.

'Yes. I trust you.' He was an exceedingly wily character but in no position to double-cross. He played tough games, but had been encouraged to believe we did, and had huge capital sunk in the country. He would not be doing us for a few thousand dollars.

He left immediately. Ben escorted him to the car, and returned, muttering about the absurdity of having so much money in brown paper parcels which he had originally assumed to contain oriental delicacies.

'Maybe Daniel can change them up into higher denominations,' he suggested.

'Some maybe, but not all,' said Daniel, who had returned from outside where he had been keeping watch.

Later that night we went through the details of the telex operation for the last time.

In the morning Ben accompanied Daniel to the bank. I went to Walker Hill.

I had breakfast with Paul, after which we went to his room where I opened my case and took out a handful of nylon stockings.

'First a corset. Now nylons,' he said. 'What's next?'

'It was Ben's idea,' I said. 'We've got to get the money out somehow.' Taking currency out of the country was an offence, viewed as seriously as bringing gold in.

His room didn't lock, so we went into the bathroom. Each stocking held eight bundles. I tied them around him, reefing them in front.

He was wrapped in three stockings when there was a knock at the door. It was Ben, with more parcels under his arm.

'Not more!' Paul exclaimed, horrified. I loaded another stocking and tried to fit it around Paul but there was no room anywhere.

'We'll have to try it like this,' Ben said. 'Put your clothes on and try walking about. How does it feel? It looks perfect.'

'I feel grossly overweight. It's going to be bloody hot too.' He didn't look at all pleased.

'Try breathing in deeply.'

'I can't.'

'Perhaps you strapped them on too tight,' Ben suggested. Paul took off his suit and Ben loosened the stockings. Paul was much happier.

'What are we going to do with the rest of the money.' I said perplexed.

Ben studied the remaining parcels a moment then said, 'We'll have to take it.'

'I haven't got any more nylons.'

'I brought some more.' Ben produced them from his jacket pockets. I stripped and he loaded me then I did the same for him. Soon after he left to catch his plane. Paul and I didn't have reservations but we left for the airport in search of possible cancellations.

We found a plane but it was delayed because of a technical fault so we spent eight hours waiting, sweating torrentially.

Eventually our flight was called and we trekked out into the searing heat of the afternoon. At last we were leaving Korea.

Chapter 11/Tokyo–Hong Kong

At Tokyo, Paul, who had not been more than a few feet away, had disappeared into thin air.

We had walked through what must be the longest maze of passenger corridors in the world and arrived at immigration control, where we had split up into different queues. These queues trailed through separate high-walled passages. Emerging the other side I had turned, expecting to link up with him, but he had gone.

I scanned the hall where our cases would arrive, but he was nowhere in sight. After fifteen minutes, there was still no sign of him. He had been stopped, that was certain. 'A carrier has to be stopped – and stripped before he is caught,' I reminded myself. There was no point in worrying, so I collected my luggage, cleared customs, and resigned myself to an indefinite wait at the terminal entrance.

'What kept you?' I asked, over three-quarters of an hour later.

'They wouldn't let me pass until I had a confirmed onward booking to Hong Kong. I've got to leave in twenty-four hours.'

'Why?'

'My disembarkation card didn't match my ticket. On the disembarkation card I'd written that my next stop was Hong Kong. The ticket said London.'

'Bloody stupid! But, according to their regulations they're undoubtedly right. Well you certainly gave them a chance to take a good look at you. Do you realise that you've risked all on something completely avoidable?'

He nodded glumly.

The episode was a good demonstration of the vital importance of paying proper attention to seemingly irrelevant details.

Our bus took us by flyover direct to the city centre. We booked in at the Hilton – which, unlike those of London, Brussels or Hong Kong, left us breathless with its elegance.

That evening I invited Paul to my room. He was the best man we had who was likely to accept the role of collector in either Zurich or Amsterdam.

How would he like to rob a bank? How would he himself like to relieve it of $300,000 in cash? How could I put it to him so that it would seem like just one natural step on from the quiet gentlemanly occupation of gold smuggling, on the long trail to Nirvana, Samadhi – eternal happiness?

First I took his mental temperature with a few general questions on how he felt about his life within the organisation then having concluded that he was totally intoxicated, metaphorically that is, I put the proposition to him.

To my amazement he accepted immediately, asking practically no questions, insisting only that no one but Ben and I should know about his participation, and agreeing to the ridiculous fee of five thousand dollars. He had no worries about the job.

The next day he had to leave for Hong Kong and, though I had originally intended to spend time making contact with some of the potential customers that Kuon and Ben had lined up, I decided to leave with him. We would have plenty of time after the coup to organise ourselves in Tokyo.

As Shirak and Karbi, in London and Brussels, would be frantic with worry at not having heard from me I dropped a short note to Tania, knowing that the contents would be relayed on: 'I am leaving here in just under an hour and will be home more or less straight away, though have to stop off for a couple of days in Hong Kong. Sorry you've been left so far away for so long. It has been unavoidable. Please tell my friend "K" that everything is okay and that this is the first day I've had the physical opportunity to write. Better to leave all news until return. There is far too much!'

In Hong Kong we booked into the President and Paul agreed to stay locked in his room, guarding the money while I contacted Ben. Apparently he had spent that morning and the whole of the previous day visiting an impressive number of the two hundred banks in the colony in an effort to change the wan but none were interested in the quantity we had or would offer more than a discount of twenty-five per cent on smaller amounts. Kuon seemed our only hope. Ben put our problem to him and called me later with instructions to meet him on the island side.

I hopped on to the Celestial Star, a double-decker ferry, with a briefcase in one hand and a suitcase in the other, gripping both for dear life. The mid-afternoon sun above Victoria Peak brought out the heavy concentration of skyscrapers in sharp relief against the steep dark mass of the island's backbone. The sparkling waters of the harbour were alive with walla walla, sampan, junk and other traffic. After a ten minute trip and a five minute walk, hustled by every rickshaw man in sight, I joined Ben at the Mandarin, where we caught a cab, which took us a mile along the waterfront past the Macao Pier to one of Kuon's warehouses.

'I have made an appointment for you at five o'clock,' Kuon said. 'You said the amount was exactly 6,220,800 wan?'

'Yes,' I replied.

'Good, good. You will be pleased to hear that I have the official exchange rate for you.'

'Two hundred and seventy to the dollar?'

He bowed.

'I shan't be coming with you, but no doubt you will have implicit trust in the arrangements I have made.'

'Complete,' I assured him.

'However, before explaining to you what to do, let me put your minds at rest. The exchange will be guaranteed by me personally.'

'That is exceptionally kind of you.'

'Anyway, you will find things perfectly straightforward. You want it in U.S. dollars, not Hong Kong?'

'Preferably – but we have no objection to the other,' I said.

'Good. Now, go to this address. It's my own fish shop. Hence the card. As you enter the street from the harbour side, you will find it on your left. Immediately opposite is a small market alley which you must go along. Approximately half way along you will come to a rattan stall, also on your left. Behind this is a rattan shop. The elder of the two gentlemen there is expecting a Mr Richard and his friend to call. You give your parcels to him. If you are obliged to wait for any long time, do not be alarmed. These gentlemen are very reliable.'

Kuon did not remind us with whom we would be dealing. He had already told us that only one buyer would be interested in what we had – the North Korean Government. The gentleman we were to meet were no doubt their agents.

'Call me when you've finished and we'll have lunch,' suggested Kuon as we left.

The place was easy to find but there was only one person on the premises. He made no reference to the parcels but simply asked us to follow him. We climbed a dingy flight of stairs and arrived in a dingier room.

'Excuse me,' he said, and disappeared through the door.

Less than a minute later he returned with four men. He took our parcels, handed them to the men, who sat down at two desks and began to count. When the counting was completed and double-checked, our host put the money back in the wrapping paper and walked out with it. His assistants followed.

In less than a minute they were back, with what I assumed to be the exact equivalent in U.S. dollars. I counted the bundles and made a quick calculation, very much doubting that any error had been made. None had.

'I do hope you will come again,' our host said. We nodded and left.

At lunch the next day we consulted Kuon.

'Is there a black market here for diamonds?' Ben asked.

'Well, there is a market, but the profit is not very considerable,' replied Kuon.

We needed to know the market, as it was into diamonds that the proceeds from the Amsterdam bank would be converted.

'Also you have to be exceedingly careful. It's a specialised business and easy for a dabbler to come unstuck. You can bring good stones in but be unable to sell – and so have your capital tied up longer than you have bargained for. I don't know the business well, but suggest, if you want to make enquiries, that you go and see my friend Mr Tsang. I would prefer that you made your own approaches, in this instance, without mentioning my name.'

Two hours later we were at Tsang's. Going into his shop knowing that he was approachable, was very different from going into another shop blind. Ben made the first tentative enquiries.

'Yes, I would be most interested to see and advise you on the disposal of any diamonds you have,' Tsang told us, 'so long as I am assured by you that they have arrived in your possession in the Colony through normal channels.'

'Naturally,' replied Ben.

Tsang, proving to be ultra cautious, refused to be led into the smallest indication of a confession that his business was not conducted other than one hundred per cent legitimately; though he was prepared to discuss other people's 'under the counter business', emphatically in the abstract and saying that he really knew very little about it. We did gather however that the easiest stones to dispose of were one-and-a-half carats, white – not blue white – with flat bottoms and tops.

Whereas the money telexed to Amsterdam would be converted into diamonds, that to Zurich would be converted into gold, which we had the manpower to transport speedily to Hong Kong where we had no worry about customers. Ben had lined up enough to absorb nine loads of twenty-four kilos per week, valued at about $360,000 U.S. Though the profit on resale would be low, this was of no consequence as we were primarily interested in the anonymous conversion of cash.

I spent the following three days in Hong Kong so that Ben could introduce me to the most important of his contacts. This meant that if anything happened to him I would be able to take over. After one of these meetings I went into the Mandarin to cool off and was in the lounge when a Chinese girl came and sat at the same table, although two chairs along. She was alone, extremely well dressed and quite beautiful. I was not interested in any playful diversion at this time, but decided to strike up a brief conversation, to which she responded admirably. Yes, she would join me for a drink.

She was there, she said, vaguely expecting a friend to arrive on the hydrofoil from Macao. Her friend failed to appear, so since I was intrigued to encounter a Chinese girl whose main passions in life were Shakespeare, Spencer and Chaucer, and whose hobbies were philosophy, sailing and bicycling round islands, I invited her for lunch. There was a further reason and it was to do with another of her hobbies, collecting precious stones, a subject on which she was extremely well informed. Over lunch I pumped her for information.

'Do you do much travelling?'

'Whenever I can. I'm going on a world trip with my family in December.'

'You must be very rich.'

'No,' she replied, 'not at all. But I manage to combine pleasure with business.'

This was interesting. Five minutes before she had informed me that she was a secretary and complained that her work never allowed her to travel much.

'Business? What business?' I asked.

'Oh, just business,' she replied.

This wasn't the bright evasion I had expected.

'Commissions,' she said; then, seeing I wasn't convinced, 'helping my father,' and, 'assignments for friends'. This was less bright still and quite out of character. So, still totally unconvinced, I decided to play a hunch.

'Well, so you like to make a mystery of it?' I began. 'If you'd been really cool, you wouldn't have made any mention of your business at all. Now you're going to have to make a revelation of it – but as far as I'm concerned, there's no mystery at all.'

I spoke slowly but forcefully, as if I was amused, but also in earnest.

'It's quite simple,' I continued, 'and you couldn't have a more elegant or innocent guise for it. You're a smuggler.'

I looked her straight in the eyes as I spoke. Perhaps she thought I was playing as her expression was one of amusement. I would have to be more exact.

'You take diamonds into Manila, that's for certain,' I said, as she had mentioned the place frequently. 'You probably do the same into Japan though I'm doubtful. Into Bangkok you probably take gold.' I felt like adding, 'But you've given up the latter for the moment because the price isn't so good,' but I stopped myself. 'The commodity is unimportant, but I've found the principle. Also you're smart and enterprising enough to operate on your own, or do you work for a boyfriend, or – let me guess – Daddy? Well, no. Daddy, I imagine, would view your antics with horror.'

She didn't fall through the floor – but she wasn't so amused any more either. I was warm.

'So now you have nothing to hide. Anyway, I'm not going to be shocked, rather interested, so tell me about it. Perhaps we can even do some business together.'

There was a long silence which as good as confirmed my

suspicions, then she said, 'No, I do it alone. But every now and again, mind you. Not as a serious business. For fun really, and it pays my expenses.'

'Very interesting. Tell me, what's the profit on taking diamonds into Manila?'

'Well, I only take in very little.'

'Well, what's the profit on this "very little"?'

'About a hundred per cent.'

'But that's fantastic. How can it be?'

'But it's true. You can check.'

'Well, with that profit, wouldn't you be interested in taking your business more seriously?'

'Not really. It would be too difficult with my job. Anyway, as I said, I do it mostly for fun. But I'll help you if you want.'

'What can you do?'

'Well, I could introduce you to a friend of mine, a Philippine minister. I stay with him in Manila. He's over here at the moment.'

'What does he do?'

'I sell to most of his friends.'

After she had told me that she had no difficulty in selling whatever she brought in and that the minister was quite happy with the occasional twenty-five per cent she paid him on transactions which involved him in no personal risk, she agreed that she would ring him that evening and speak to me again afterwards.

It was late the following afternoon when I saw Blue Cloud (the literal translation of her name) again. As arranged she took me to the minister, who confirmed everything she had said. I had no intention of paying him twenty-five per cent on the quantity we anticipated, but decided to leave negotiations until we were ready to do business. Establishing contact and being assured of a market were sufficient at this point.

The Far East is a truly amazing place. It seemed to me, from my brief experience, that everybody, in all walks of life, was involved in some kind of racket. It struck me as an interesting coincidence that on the very day that I was meeting a Philippine minister, Ben was meeting another Philippine minister not far away: one who had a considerably more ambitious scheme. With an interest in a large shipping company, he was preparing to scuttle one of his own ships, and was seeking a third party who would agree to have purchased the cargo on board, for which the proof of payments would be supplied by him. The percentage of the insurance proceeds which he was offering, for this small part, was close to a million dollars. Ben was asked to consider the offer, but we were not interested.

I was in Hong Kong over a week. Ben had excellent contacts and we encountered several similar propositions every day. I concluded that a man with little capital and no scruples could not fail to find the place one of boundless opportunities. Our major asset, due entirely to Ben's continuous and magnificent public relations work, was that we had been convincingly projected as the likeable bosses of a thoroughly reliable and efficient organisation, rich in resources of capital and manpower, that carried on its own several businesses successfully and at the same time were always open to anything. The more I thought about this, and the staggering goodwill capital built up by Ben out of all proportion to what we were, the more I realised how important it was to return to Hong Kong, even be based there, to make full use of it. These thoughts brought me back once again to the problem of Shirak. We could do no serious business with him as a partner.

Chapter 12/Brussels: Double-double-cross

Shirak was going to be 'double-crossed'. At least this was the word he would have used, had he known what was about to take place. As a dangerously unreliable and destructive ingredient, a threat to our security and therefore our survival, it was agreed that he be removed from practical involvement in our organisation; but it was also agreed that his removal be conducted in the most gentlemanly manner possible and that though completely out we would continue to honour our original financial agreement – despite the heavy loss that this would entail.

Getting him to agree to all this was going to be one hell of a problem. Shirak, suffering loss of face or suspecting that he was being manipulated or taken advantage of, was bound to be a very wild man. Although Ben agreed that his removal was a necessity, he viewed the prospect as hopeless and feared the consequences of an attempt. However, he would be several thousand miles away and he had left the moves up to me. To avoid any confusion he agreed to have all the calls coming from England blocked, except those from my agreed pseudonym.

Getting rid of Shirak was not just a personal problem, but linked with a financial one.

First, both he and Karbi would expect a report.

They would quite rightly be expecting glowing forecasts and some immediate concrete plans to be put into effect: one carrier a week going into Korea, or at least two a week into Tokyo or, until then, six carriers a week going into Hong Kong. Something like that. But in fact, it was imperative for my plan that all operations be immediately suspended. It was also inconceivable that the details of our telex operation be confided to a single soul who was not directly involved. Therefore I could not report success.

Nor could I report failure. Firstly it would not be believed. Secondly it would result in the organisation being liquidated: okay, but not with capital having to be returned and profits shared out, which would be demanded immediately, at a time when we had a vital need of all available capital.

What report could I give? The problem seemed insoluble.

How would Karbi respond to my proposition that his kid brother be removed? As much as he hated him, might he not feel that such a move would endanger his own position?

Even if Karbi responded favourably, how would Shirak react? Would he tolerate the thought of anyone else running 'his' organisation, while he himself had no authoritative part? On the formidable evidences of all past performances, he would not.

Paul and I had left Ben in Hong Kong, boarding the same Lufthansa flight, chasing twilight around the globe and bound for Brussels. I had only a few weeks in which to prepare for the telex operation, which had to be put into motion immediately. Liquidation would have to begin and the Shirak situation resolved within a couple of days, or I would have no freedom to work. As for the Shirak situation I had only a few hours in which to make up my mind before confronting Karbi and being thrown into the thick of it. There could be no dithering once I had arrived. By the time we reached Frankfurt, to change from our Boeing 707 to a Caravelle, time had become desperately short. The situation would have to be played by ear.

I decided that I would postpone my meeting with Karbi and avoid having him breathing down my neck, by booking into the Atlanta Hotel instead of returning to our base; also that Paul had to blow himself ostensibly from the organisation – and I had to prevent him being pumped.

'Paul,' I said, 'one of the first points you must put across is that you are leaving the organisation for three to four months for a long overdue visit to your mother in Australia. If asked why you have bothered to return to Europe, you can say that you have done so to collect your personal belongings and to sell your Porsche and vintage Riley in London. It's advisable from now on that everybody imagines you to be ten thousand miles away and off the scene.

'I'll give you a few minutes to arrive at the flat,' I continued, 'then I'm going to telephone Karbi. Karbi will doubtless be round to see me at the speed of lightning, but make sure that Tania is with him.'

Tania's presence would keep our exchanges at a reasonably non-committal and superficial level, and act as a check against Karbi's penetrations, giving me time to take a thermal reading of his frame of mind as well as things in general. He would know, or be reminded of the fact, that business was never discussed in front of her or anyone else.

'As soon as they have left you are to inform the two boys there that I want to see them together later in the day but that I don't want Karbi to know about the meeting.'

'When do we return to London?' Paul asked.

'Tomorrow. Remember, if asked anything whatsoever, you know absolutely nothing – except that we sold the gold in Korea and about your own experience as a carrier.' I had no idea which way Karbi would respond to my propositions but wasn't unduly worried – the business couldn't exist without Ben and myself, so in reality Karbi had very little choice.

I booked into a double room and they arrived shortly afterwards, Tania bouncing with joy and Karbi betraying simmering undercurrents of hostility.

'Did you get a good price?' he asked.

'Yes,' I replied. 'But unfortunately it's out of the question going back there', and I explained why.

'Why didn't you write to let us know what was going on?' he asked, anger imminent.

'For the reasons I gave you before I left here and for the

reasons I gave you before we left Hong Kong, *and* as per Ben's warnings, all made perfectly clear,' I replied. 'Communications are too dangerous, as they are all monitored.'

I gave a general account of conditions in Korea, emphasising the hazards we had survived and the problems we had surmounted; followed by a glowing report on conditions in Tokyo and Hong Kong where we had business lined up, and mention of the fact that I had returned with several propositions.

'What the hell were we supposed to do here? How the hell were we supposed to know what was going on?'

'Well, you knew exactly what you were supposed to do. And no news was to be taken as good news, wasn't it? All things were clearly established.'

'Shirak has been going beserk, completely losing control of himself several times, once threatening to kill Adam and almost doing so.'

I heard an account of this scene later:

'Don't kill me. Don't kill me,' Adam had pleaded, cowing in absolute terror in a corner of the office, as Shirak had just crushed a glass in his hand and his blood was splashing all over the place.

Then he had given up, just moaning to himself, 'This is the end. I knew it would come like this,' and folded himself up into oblivion for the end that finally didn't come.

'If ever I have the slightest suspicion that you're involved in any attempt to double-cross me, you know exactly what will happen to you,' Shirak had told Adam and left.

'I'll come to the question of Shirak later,' I said to Karbi.

'I've stood alone magnificently and bravely, holding everything together this end, and the London end,' Karbi implied in so many words. Tania didn't volunteer to back him up.

She did, however, volunteer to wait downstairs to enable us to talk more freely.

'Life with Karbi has been hell,' she said, as I took her to the lift. 'He's been going out of his mind. Every day, sometimes twice a day, he's been going down to the airport, expecting you. In fact he's been utterly unbearable and shitty. That's not all. I'm warning you. He's been trying to take over.'

'Impossible,' I said. 'Can you prove that?'

'Certainly.'

This put a new light on things. I accepted Tania's word and returned to Karbi, knowing precisely what course of action I would take. I would not confide our telex scheme to him. I would not involve him in future gold operations. He would be eliminated from the organisation. However, I couldn't remove him overnight or the damage he would do, with the list of our carriers' names and other information, would be irreparable.

'Well, what's news?' he began.

'First of all, exactly as I've already told you. We made close to seventy-five per cent gross profit on our sale in Korea. I have, for your interest, a tape of the transaction from beginning to end.'

'Well,' I said, having given him a complete account of all events and situations to do with gold, omitting only the names and descriptions of our contacts, particularly that of Daniel Grand at the Bank of America. 'Any questions so far?'

Silence.

'What about the propositions?' he asked.

'I'll come to those in a minute. We'll get "business done" out of the way first, then we can discuss what is to come. Any questions?'

There was another long pause.

'Why, you look quite peevish,' I said. 'What's up?'

'Why no communication for three whole weeks? I can't understand it,' he repeated for the umpteenth time.

I answered as previously.

'I opened your letter to Tania,' he said, after a further painful lapse of time.

'Why?' I asked coldly.

'I wanted to know what was going on.'

You're amazing me. And what did you imagine was going on? And if there was anything going on, do you really think I would be so foolish as to have written anything of it to Tania? When you are anyway bound to ask her to show it to you?'

'It was possible.'

'No business is possible at all', I said, about to express my thorough fed-upness, 'if everybody is going to be full of paranoic complexes about things going on behind their backs. What is more, if you do not trust either Ben or myself then you should quit the business. If you don't do so then I will, because any decision to go on would be nonsensical.'

'I've learnt a great deal about you since you've been away,' he said, later on, obviously launching into some kind of attack.

'Good,' I said. 'I've hidden nothing about myself. Please spout.'

Lying back on the bed, I waited for him to carry on. He paced ponderously up and down the room, with his eyes protruding and a tight expression on his face.

'Your friends', he said, 'are not as loyal as you think.'

'Oh? . . . ' I questioned in a long drawn out utterance that ended conspicuously on a higher note than it had begun. I could afford to be playful, having been totally straight forward in my dealings up until that moment.

'Oh yes,' he echoed, but on the same low notes and in a way which suggested that these very two words themselves proved the fact. 'I've learnt some very interesting things.'

'Go on.'

'Things have been going on behind my back. And I don't like it.'

This line of attack was bound to prove most useful. He was making a big mistake and it was one which would put him at an immense psychological disadvantage.

'Well, let's have all these startling discoveries of conspiracies.'

'I don't like the way you treat me,' he said, dropping his original line and beginning another.

'You must be joking. I have always treated you excellently. At this moment for reasons unknown to me, you are making a bloody fool of yourself.

'Anyway,' I concluded, 'so far you have made cryptic accusations without substantiating one. But what really is on your mind? Whatever it is, for Christ's sake get it off – because it seems to me like shit.'

'I still don't like the way you treat me,' he repeated, absolutely enraged and becoming less and less distinguishable from a wild Shirak.

He approached menacingly across the room, looking as if he was going to hit me. I remained as I was. He grabbed the lapels of my jacket with one hand and raised the other threateningly above my head.

'Well go on. Hit me. I'm not going to move. Actually I'll stand up and you can get a better shot – but what will that prove? Only that you're no better than your brother. Personally I think we've got no future together and had better pack it up.'

Pack up? Bloody likely! He relaxed his grip.

'Haven't I always treated you as a friend? And remember one thing – wasn't it I who schemed to have you working with us in the first place? As for today, either you've invented what's in your mind, for whatever devious reasons, or you really believe you have some genuine facts. Give them to me. Your silence only makes your behaviour seem worse.'

'What about the propositions?'

'There are none which concern any of us until this situation is resolved.'

'Well,' he began, again after much thought. 'I know about your secret correspondence.'

'Oh yes? What secret correspondence? And with whom?'

'Your secret correspondence with Ben.'

'Go on.'

'Your correspondence with Ben in London.'

'Aren't all letters arriving in London first of all received by Shirak, then relayed to me, then available for your perusal?'

'What about those going to your private address, Court-field Gardens? Collected by Adam.'

'What of them?'

'All addressed to you in some other name,' he continued.

'Go on,' I encouraged, beginning to see the picture. 'Which name of mine?'

'Patrick Leander,' he said, lingering on the words, with a twinkle in his eye and all teed up for victory.

'Supposing you tell me about those letters,' I began. 'I'll tell you this, you raving idiot. You've discovered nothing. Nothing that is not clearly typed out in "London Office Procedures" – which it appears you have not read. Adam's first instructions every morning are to go to Courtfield Gardens, and other places, and to collect mail to this and other mysterious people and to place it in my file at the office. If this is so secret, why are the instructions typed out for all to see?'

'Why then do you use the name Patrick Leander?'

'It's quite simple. All letters addressed in my name are opened by London Office, because they pertain to business, and so that they can be processed in my absence. Now what happens to my personal mail? Here, read this. It's addressed to Leander and you will see it's from my sister in Africa. Now dial my supposedly betraying friend Adam and ask whether he has ever collected any mysterious Leander mail from anywhere in the Far East.'

He was shattered.

'This is an utterly straightforward business. Utterly simple. Well I've wasted enough time dealing with a bunch of psychopaths, kids and idiots. I've had enough. The rubbish has got to be cut out. Some people have got to go. We'll discuss that this afternoon. Now leave.'

'What!' he exclaimed. He had certainly not been treated like this before.

'Leave. Go and clean up your mind. Then come back. Tania is downstairs. Ask her to come up.'

He objected. I insisted. His position had dwindled to very little.

'Are you going to ring Shirak?'

'Not until we've had a further talk. But he's got to go for a start – as you yourself suggested some time ago. Now think about that. Either this or we break up. We've got contacts arriving in from the Far East. Can you imagine him handling them? There's a whole load of changes that must take place – from today onwards. But don't worry, I'm not going to be doing anything without you – that is, after you've pulled your socks up.'

As soon as Karbi had left, I telephoned the two boys, Phillip and Peter, and asked them to come round immediately. I would be needing them both for parts in the telex operation, but as far as Karbi was concerned they had to be blown.

Tania came up, and I listened to her account of things in my absence. Karbi had pulled every devious trick in the book in order first to undermine the loyalties of those who were aligned with me, then to take over. He had not spared Tania in this exercise. He had been right about one thing: a lot of changes were going to take place when Roderic came back!

'The dramatic changes about which you have been so accurately forewarned,' I said to the boys, enjoying the irony, 'are now about to take place. We have raised a buying capital of a quarter of a million U.S. dollars and will be running two routes,' I said to them, after filling them in on my intentions regarding Shirak and Karbi and instructing them on what precautions to take. I had also thought it advisable to indicate that we already had the capital so that should the telex coup be publicised they would not think of relating this to our sudden wealth. 'You, Phillip, will be our buyer in Geneva. You, Peter, will be assisting our buyer in Brussels.' I told them separately, 'I'll visit you both in about three days and discuss the details with you.'

Within two hours they had left for England.

I rang Adam.

'Everything is in a mess. Shirak is storming. I have been instructed to take no instructions from you whatsoever.'

'Well, that's your choice. But you had better choose again now, because Shirak is being kicked out.'

'Well that's something I don't want to know anything about. He has already threatened to kill me twice.'

'Yes, I know. Well, okay. In that case forget I have said anything. As far as anybody is concerned I haven't even phoned you, and I won't disturb your mind by telling you that Karbi is due out as well.'

'Please don't. I couldn't take it.'

Karbi returned in the early evening, a reformed man. He had realised his utter dependency and was intent on salvaging his position in my eyes and demonstrating that he was not the kind of fellow I must have thought him from his recent behaviour and how invaluable his services would prove to be in the future. I listened to his various tunes bearing these messages.

Karbi was fundamentally the only person in the world whom Shirak trusted. Only he could persuade Shirak to accept my terms and convince him that we would continue to honour our financial obligations to him in full. They would both have to be told that some deal was on the verge of taking place, without being given any details of it. However, whereas Shirak might be persuaded to remove himself from the scene, Karbi would expect to be given a clear outline of the future and to be immediately involved in something. Therefore it occurred to me that the best thing to do, until the time came for wrenching the carpet from under his feet, would be to feed him the details of a purely fantasy proposition. 'If he later decides to seek revenge through "squealing",' I thought, 'then let it be with information which is going to make him look ridiculous and lead him on a wild goose chase.'

'The only thing I can tell you about the deal.' I said, 'is that a minor clerk in Hong Kong has found a way to do up a bank and is intending to do so to the tune of $350,000. I can't give you any other information except that he's using cashier's cheques and other forged documents, needs co-operation which a friend of Ben's is arranging the other end, as Ben himself naturally cannot ever be seen within a mile of him, and that it is advisable for the proceeds to be transferred out of the Colony the same day.'

'What's our cut?'

'Two-thirds,' I said.

'What do we have to do?'

'As I said, all we have to do is to arrange the collection in London – and find a man to do it naturally. This is literally all I can tell you.'

'Are you sure it's on?'

'Definitely.'

'When?'

'At the end of the second week in August.'

This was the first instalment of the deal. I had time to work out later how it would develop from there.

'Now you understand,' I said, 'why your brother must know absolutely nothing. You know his problem keeping things to himself. Don't tell him any more than that the deal is on, and he'll have to trust your assurance of the fact.'

'Shirak', he said, 'will not accept rejection on any grounds. You know that.'

'Well, either I go or he goes. Make your choice.'

After long thinking, he asked, 'Do you trust me?'

'Yes, I trust you.' I replied.

'Then leave the matter to me. Don't ask any questions. I'll handle Shirak. I know how to do it.'

'I promise everything will be all right,' he continued. 'But you must put your decision to him when you arrive in London.'

This sudden confidence was news to me. Assuring me that he could predict as well as control the reactions of his brother when previously he had lived in fear of him, was a mysterious change which seemed only accountable by the fact that some conspiratorial relationship had developed between them.

'Are you really sure?' I asked, as silence before such an obvious change in things might have put him on his guard.

'I don't think I'll have any difficulty.'

'Just make it clear that my mind is made up. Also emphasise that this is a matter of business expediency and nothing personal. Our kind of business cannot be carried out with his kind of interferences. It is simply not possible to work with him as an active partner.'

'Why do we have to close down operations?'

'Because of the London-Hong Kong link in this deal and the fact that your brother has been opening his mouth too much.

'We don't want any of our carriers known, let alone questioned. We can never use any of our boys again. We have to blow the lot of them. In three to four months' time we'll have to start our recruiting from scratch.'

'What about Adam?' he asked.

'Ah! The loyal Adam. I'll take your word that his loyalties are so skin deep. In which case, I have no further use for him. You can use him if you like, but not when I'm around.'

The next day Tania, Paul and I were to catch the Ostend-Dover ferry, Karbi would stay in Brussels to tidy up our affairs, then he would spend a few days in London before going on a short visit to his family in Norway. 'What are you going to be doing?' he asked.

'Tania and I will be going to Ireland for a few weeks. We may even get married there.'

'Oh!' he jumped, 'If you're going to get married, I want to be there.'

'Damn it!' I thought, 'Just when I thought I'd got rid of him.'

Chapter 13/London

Visions of pot-smokers tortured on racks and hung in their cells encouraged Adam in his belief that to be the subject of police interrogation was a fate worse than death. With traces of paranoia perhaps, he had a vivid and over-active imagination.

His response therefore to my blunt opening – 'We have a plan to do up a bank for $600,000,' – was predictably anelectric. And the kind of expression I got when I suggested that he might have a useful part to play in this was one a pregnant cow might give if asked to run in a steeplechase marathon. Sighs, shudders, and icicle grins followed as I unfolded the full horrors. First the news of Shirak's ousting hanging over his head like the old sword of Damocles, now this:

'He'll get me,' he persisted.

'All you have to do is keep out of the way.'

'Don't worry. I will.'

Having covered the main cause for his concern, we returned to the proposition. Unlike Paul, Adam wanted to know every aspect and bombarded me with questions. I repeated the theory a dozen times and invited him to pull as many holes in it as possible, believing that his inability to do so would be reassuring.

'If ever I was caught the scandal would kill my father,' he said.

'It would resurrect him. Why? Is he ill?'

'No, just the shock would kill him.'

'Does he have a weak heart?'

'Not that I know of.'

'Then he could get over it.'

Adam gave his acceptance, but it was too tentative for my liking.

'That's not good enough,' I said. 'If you're not dead convinced, forget about it.'

I gave him the remainder of the day to think about it, but we continued discussions as if he had already decided.

'How much will I be collecting?' he asked for the third time, obviously leading to something.

'A hundred-and-fifty thousand dollars on the Friday and the same again on the Monday.'

'And I get five thousand pounds?' he queried. This was already more than Paul's five thousand dollars.

'For both. Not each,' I emphasised. 'You think that's not enough?'

'It's definitely not much in relation to what's being drawn out. Is it?'

'You can do what the other fellow's doing. Invest it with us in diamonds and I'll guarantee you ten thousand pounds. You'll get plenty of other opportunities.'

After a while he accepted. Our meeting had lasted the whole morning.

It was time to call on Shirak. I mounted the stairs to his flat, with trepidation.

'Good morning, sir!' he greeted me, in whimsical fashion, his bulging brown eyes expressing nothing I could readily interpret, and on his lips the trace of a smile. 'And how are *you*?'

Good so far, I thought.

Sherkasian zombies were bathing in the blessed sun of their Lord and Master waiting for the next command that would make their presences both felt and useful.

'Out,' he said. 'All of you.' They scampered out.

'And where the bloody hell have you been?' he turned to me belligerently. Belligerency being his natural state, I found nothing unusual in this.

'What do you mean, where the bloody hell have *I* been? Where the bloody hell have *you* been? I've been leaving messages for you all over the place.'

All was friendly!

'Where's the money?' he asked. A poignant shot!

'It's safe in a bank in Hong Kong. I've come back with about two thousand. If you want detailed accounts you can have them at any time. However, unless you desperately want money for any reason, it's best left where it is.'

I gave him a five minute account of our activities and began launching into prepared themes. I had hardly done so, when I was stopped.

'Okay, so you're telling me that I'm no good,' he said. 'I know it. I'm wrong.'

'That's about it,' I replied, amazed at his capitulation.

'What do you want to suggest then?'

'The partnership goes on, but in the division of profits only. You have nothing whatsoever to do with the running of the business . . . '

'Okay. As you say. You're the boss.'

'I must say, I'm amazed you've taken everything so well. I was expecting tirades of abuse, but you seem not a bit surprised. What's up? Why so happy?'

'Well, we'll do other business together,' he said.

'No reason why not.'

'I'm buying a hotel.'

'Oh yeah? With what?'

'With the money you're going to give me.'

He smiled. Karbi, for reasons unknown to me, had succeeded in working a minor miracle.

'You trust Karbi to look after your interests?'

'He'll do what I tell him.'

Leaving Shirak, I went directly to the Chelsea Potter. I needed passports for Paul and Adam, which had to be obtained by people unconnected with us.

The first prospect was a 'hippy' one who used the Potter as his lunchtime club.

'I'm quite serious,' I said. 'For how much would you be willing to shave off your hyacinth locks?'

'At least something sufficient to send me off for a recovery in the South of France.'

'Would fifty pounds be enough? All you have to do is have your photograph taken and keep your mouth shut.'

'Done.'

We shook hands on the deal, and he made a confession.

'I'm bald,' he said, 'quite bald.'

I looked at him, staggered.

'Well, that's no good. Here, take a couple of tenners and go and buy a wig. I'll meet you back here at six.'

That done, I found applicant number two. At the Bunch of Grapes, near Beauchamp Place. My doubts about him were cast aside by the fact that he was returning to Malawi in a couple of weeks. I sent him to have his hair cut and photographs taken.

The photographs of both of them would be on files, so it was necessary that they be either unrecognisable or untraceable. Neither of them had form of any sort.

Already somebody had been despatched to Somerset House to collect two birth certificates. The names on these were 'John Brown' and 'Percy Fox'.

Paul and Adam using these two names, produced signatures *in their ordinary handwriting* which I gave to Hippy and Malawi, who practised until they could reproduce them fluently. Hippy had a natural flair for forgery and reproduced a beautiful specimen instantly, but one hour had to be spent advising Malawi before he could produce anything adequate.

The following morning, Hippy went under his own steam to a Labour Exchange, with the birth certificate and three photographs. Adam and I took Malawi to another, dropping him off a couple of hundred yards away. He emerged after a few minutes, and we picked him up as soon as he was well clear of the building. He had the document all right, but it was a disaster. The clerk had fairly soused the photograph in glue before pasting it on and the dye of the official stamp had run so that the printing had become completely disfigured. It was the real thing, but unpresentable, and the job had to be done again.

I left Adam in charge of the next effort and collected Hippy's work. It was satisfactory and I paid him off. Later, back at the flat, I studied the passport more carefully and wondered if it wasn't too good. The official stamp was so sharply outlined that I doubted my ability to reproduce the half of it that would be torn off before the replacement of Paul's photograph.

A couple of hours later, a very perplexed Adam arrived.

'Where's the passport?' I asked.

'I haven't got it.'

'Why not? What happened?'

'I went to another Labour Exchange and dropped him, then I waited for half an hour, but he didn't show so I went in to look for him and he wasn't there.'

'He wasn't there?'

'I looked everywhere for him. Then I went back to the car and waited another half hour but he didn't come out. I suppose he must have had some trouble.'

'Obviously. Why didn't you park outside?'

'Too conspicuous.'

'Well, we've got to have that passport today. Go to the Bunch and wait for him. Wait there all day even if the place closes.'

Adam rang me from the pub less than an hour later. Malawi was there and he didn't have the passport. I went to see him.

'Well I went in there', he explained, 'and gave the clerk the signed application. Then when she was writing out the passport she turned the birth certificate over and asked me if I had applied for a passport recently, I said 'No' and she said. 'Well what are those numbers then?' I told her that I didn't put them there and she said, 'I'll have to check with central office, maybe someone else has applied in your name.'

Naturally I froze stupid then grabbed the photos and the certificate and ran. Baby, did I run. I was running up the road so fast I ran right into a policeman. I didn't see him until it was too late. Smashed him straight into a wall. Then there were others in a car. I dashed down a tube station and jumped onto a train. Caught it by a split second.'

'Damn,' I. said. 'Now we'll have to get another birth certificate.'

We dashed to Somerset House where an accomplice insisted on having the certificate immediately instead of waiting the customary twenty-four hours. The name on this one was 'John Nicholas Robinson'. Adam wrote out a signature which Malawi practised in the car as I drove to a third Labour Exchange. We arrived a few seconds before closing time. Malawi raced in clutching his documents and photographs. The doors closed behind him. This time he would have to do the job properly.

Ben had told me that a Mr George Wakeman would 'fly anywhere in the world that I asked him to, without asking why'. This seemed a bit far-fetched but I would soon find out. If what Ben said was true then he was the ideal man to be 'John Stevenson', the person who would send the cables from Hong Kong. He could be persuaded to send them without being given any idea why, and in a way which would appear to him as if for a bona fide business reason, so that if any subsequent difficulties arose he could easily prove his innocence.

I drove down to Bournemouth to meet him, introducing myself as a friend of Ben who was passing through on my way back from Cornwall and had been asked to deliver greetings. He was a man of sixty, with, as Ben said, a great zest for living. We made small talk for about fifteen minutes then I said:

'Ben would like you to go to Hong Kong. He says you

E

need a holiday and that I am to give you a return ticket. Are you interested?'

'Yes,' he replied, almost before I had finished. 'How soon should I go?'

'In two days,' I said, 'I'll have you collected and taken to the airport.'

I left soon afterwards to see carriers, Phillip and Peter, who lived within ten miles of each other, in the same district. I told Phillip that I wanted him to drive me around the continent for four weeks after which he would become our gold buyer in Geneva on a wage of £100 a week, with an additional £100 a week expenses; and Peter that I would be needing him in Brussels.

Back in London I learnt that Karbi had just come back from Brussels and was frantic to see me.

'What's happened to the things in the Hyde Park office?' he asked.

'I've cleared it up as you've cleared up the Brussels one I hope. All the gear is in storage. We can't have it lying around and we won't be needing it for a few months.'

He was satisfied.

'What help do you need with the bank job?' he asked.

'None really. Not just yet.'

'Surely there's something I can do?'

'One major item to be taken care of is finding a man to draw from the Bank,' I said, 'I've just come back from seeing one in the Midlands. He's willing but I'm not so sure that he's suitable. Perhaps you can suggest another?'

'Belman,' he suggested, to my horror. A brainless henchman's of Shirak.

'Okay,' I said, grateful to have found something with which he could occupy himself. 'But you'll have to discuss that with Shirak without confiding in him exactly why we want him. He mustn't know anything.'

It was while listening to this discussion with Shirak that I realised how thoroughly convinced Karbi had become.

Later, having explained to him how the proceeds would be converted into diamonds, I told him that if he really wanted to do something useful he could go to Hatton Garden and establish contact with dealers there. He didn't like this idea at all, making excuses which, against the background of his earlier pleas, caused him some embarrassment.

'Okay, I'll do this myself then,' I said, imagining that the yap had now been taken out of him for some time.

Our Brussels and London offices had now been cleared and all the carriers dismissed before the eyes of Shirak and Karbi.

'Mr Stevenson' had been collected and despatched to Hong Kong. A carrier, Robert Wyndham, had been briefed to despatch other carriers from London, although as yet he had no office. Adam had left for Zurich.

It was three weeks and five days to D Day.

Karbi flew out to Norway and as far as he was concerned I would be leaving the same day for Dublin. Instead, Paul, Tania, Phillip and I drove to Dover to catch a ferry to Ostend, bound for Amsterdam, Brussels, Zurich and Geneva.

Chapter 14/Amsterdam–Zurich:
The Collectors

Even the most carefully planned operation can be thrown by unpredictable factors. We came across three. The first was fog in mid-Channel, which brought us to a halt; the second was the Ostend-Brussels autobahn, all six lanes of which had inexplicably been given over to coastbound traffic; the third was an also inexplicably Alice in Wonderland scene in which every signpost pointed to the same town simultaneously in opposite directions. We finally arrived at Bruges, a through point, over four hours late.

Eventually, thoroughly exhausted, we reached Amsterdam. A picturesque and bustling city, built around canals. Every first- and second-class hotel was fully booked. This caused some concern as it was important to find good accommodation for Paul. After a two hour search, however, we came across nothing better than a cheap pension.

When he had checked in I sent Tania off to dinner with Phillip while Paul and I drove around the city to find our bearings and specifically to look at the two banks which would soon have us as clients: the Bank of America from which we would be withdrawing the money, and the First National City Bank from which the same money would be telexed anonymously back to Hong Kong. They were a few hundred yards apart on the Herengracht, The Gentleman's Canal, both small and unimpressive.

'Don't worry,' I said to Paul who was obviously surprised. 'They might look like this but they handle millions of dollars weekly. Most of their business will be with letters of credit and general finance, not with cash accounts, but that doesn't matter. If they don't have the cash they'll write you out a cashier's cheque which you can exchange at any other bank.

Alternatively, you can give them a day's notice and they'll have it ready.'

After our tour we went to a bistrot for dinner and I gave him a further briefing, concentrating this time on his relationship with the Bank Manager.

'When the first cables arrive, you can make as much noise as you like. If you create a storm, it will be to your advantage; any suspicions they have will be proved groundless in ten days. There will be a number of transfers, remember, and each will be okay so by the time of 'main event' they will be familiar with you. Now, when you first approach the bank you will have to give some kind of explanations. Simply say that you require the cash for diamond purchases to meet flights to the Far East. Apart from explaining your urgency, it will also be the reason why you want to draw such large sums.

'The main object is to make sure that the Manager knows who you are. You are not Mr Bloggs, an anonymous customer. You are conducting big business on behalf of your partner in Hong Kong. Establish your personality. Demand good service. He won't query the nature of your business. It's not his concern whether or not you're smuggling. You will not be committing any offence in Holland. He wants your business and will be making good commissions, and, as far as he is concerned, you can always take your business elsewhere.

'Always be impeccably dressed. You're an English gentleman. Watch your accent. Let him know you're settling in Amsterdam. Ask his advice about things. Anything. Where to find a flat for example. Just don't be anonymous. When $150,000 comes into his bank and has to be paid out in cash, you don't want him suddenly to sit up and say "Who the hell's Mr Robinson?" He doesn't have to like you. He just has to know who you are.

'As for diamonds: eat them, breathe them and sleep

them. Drag yourself through the equivalent of a university course. Meet everybody in the trade. Any knowledge you acquire on the subject may be useful in the future. You can openly present yourself as a novice. Deal only with the most reputable dealers. They can't afford to sell you other than what they claim to be selling. Remember, buy only three-quarters to one and a half carat white stones, flawless, with flat, not pointed, bottoms. Nothing else.

'Have an active social life by all means while you're here but don't contact any friends in London. For the next four weeks you are, without any exception, "John Nicholas Robinson".'

Paul listened carefully to the briefing and had no doubts that he could act the role. He was only twenty-three, but looked twenty-seven and his confidence was unbounded. I didn't doubt that he could do the job – so long as he followed instructions and did not get into any situation that called for too much initiative.

At one the next day Phillip, Tania and myself left Amsterdam, heading south. We stopped in Brussels, to collect two cases and a black metal box containing equipment and documents, which had been delivered to a friend of Tania's for safe keeping. Afterwards I telephoned Adam in Zurich, Paul in Amsterdam and Ben in Hong Kong.

Adam was worried, dead worried.

'I had trouble with the police coming across the border,' he said.

'What trouble?'

'Twice they made me fill in forms.'

'So what? That's normal.'

'Well, so there's a record of my entry.'

'So what? You used the name "John Brown", didn't you?'

'No, I didn't. I changed my mind.'

'Then you're a bloody fool. Why can't you act on instructions?'

'I was the only Englishman on the train,' he sobbed. 'They're bound to be able to trace me.'

The message wasn't disturbing, but Adam's panic was.

'You can tell me the facts when I see you. Did the ten thousand dollars arrive?'

'No, it didn't.'

'Oh,' I said surprised. 'Anyway there's nothing to worry about on that score. It should be there in the morning. I'll check what time it was sent off. Meanwhile, don't worry. Just relax. We'll be with you tomorrow. Go out and enjoy the town. Get to know the place.'

'But there's nothing to do.'

'Take a boat out on the lake or something.'

'Nobody speaks a word of English.'

'Nonsense, there are plenty who do.'

Next I telephoned Paul.

'Have you found a proper hotel?' I asked.

'Not yet.'

'Have you opened an account at the bank?'

'Yes.'

'How did things go?'

'Well.'

'Okay,' I said. 'Ten thousand dollars will be arriving in the morning, from "Mr Stevenson" in Hong Kong. Leave five hundred dollars in the account, but draw out the rest, take it to to the First National City Bank and send it back to Ben. Use the name "James Sydney".'

I telephoned Ben and gave him Paul's address and confirmed his pseudonym, 'John Nicholas Robinson', and then asked him about the ten thousand dollars which Adam should have received.

'It was sent by urgent telex last Friday at three o'clock from the Hang Seng,' he said.

'Are you one hundred per cent certain it was telexed direct to the Bank of America and was not routed some other way?'

'A hundred per cent.'

'Okay, we'll see what happens tomorrow.'

'How did things go with Shirak?'

'Perfectly smoothly. He'll be no trouble. But avoid contact. One wrong word could be enough to trigger him off. He thinks I'm in Ireland.'

It was approaching midnight. We had intended to drive through the night, but exhaustion beat us and we booked into the hotel Atlanta. At five we were up and soon on our way. It took eleven hours to reach Zurich. I told Phillip and Tania to get something to eat and telephoned Adam who I arranged to meet at the station. Then I took up a position from which I could see him approach – an habitual precaution, against the unlikely event of being tailed.

We went to a café. He was very tense.

'How I hate the Swiss,' he said, 'the German Swiss.'

'Otherwise how are you?' I asked after the topics of the Swiss and Zurich had been exhausted, and I felt sufficiently safe in talking in the cafe.

'Terrible. Everything's fucked up. First of all, I've lost all my money.'

'What do you mean, "lost it"?'

'Well I must have had it picked out of my back pocket last night at the railway station.'

'What about this business of entry? Give me the facts from beginning to end. You took the train from Calais to Paris and there you changed trains for Zurich, arriving at Zurich having passed through Germany. You say you were made to fill in forms by the Swiss police?'

'Yes.'

'What time did the train leave Paris?'

'Ten past ten, the night train.'

'And what time did you arrive in Zurich?'

'Ten-thirty.'

'When were you given the forms to fill in?'

'They were already on the seat when I boarded the train.

I didn't fill them in. Then this official came to collect them and asked me why I hadn't filled them in. I pretended not to understand and he came back with two more officials. They were police forms. They're bound to remember me.'

'What language were these forms in?'

'One was in French and the other in German?'

'And when were you asked to fill them in?'

'About dawn.'

'And you went via Stuttgart?'

'Yes.'

'Well, in that case. All this took place at the French-German border and what you filled in were merely customs declaration forms. Did you fill in any more forms after this?'

'No.'

'In that case, you filled in nothing before entering Switzerland.'

It took almost an hour before all cause for further anxiety on the subject was eliminated.

'Have you seen the manager yet?' I asked.

'No, listen, I'm not going to tell him I'm a gold buyer. I'm an art dealer.'

'What the hell do you know about pictures?'

'Nothing.'

'Well what's going to happen to your front when you discover that art's his special interest?'

He shrugged his shoulders.

'Do you realise that this is the off-season for dealing? Which means that most of the galleries will be closed.'

'Oh!'

'Also,' I continued, 'isn't buying paintings on behalf of a client in Hong Kong a bit far-fetched in the middle of the off-season? And, if you're buying paintings, why do you need cash? Why aren't you paying by cheque?'

He looked at me blankly.

'Haven't you understood yet that buying gold in Switzerland is like buying cheese, that it's paid for in cash, that the banks who sell it respect their clients' wishes for anonymity, and that this very fact will protect you from any probing questions?'

We argued for a further thirty minutes, but he refused to budge.

'Okay, art dealer it is,' I said, closing the discussion.

But Adam's problems were not over yet. In the loneliness of his room he had allowed his imagination to run riot. He told me that he truly believed that once he had withdrawn the money and handed it over he was going to be liquidated.

'Liquidated?' I asked. 'What do you mean?'

'Done in,' he said.

Such a possibility might reasonably have occurred to anyone in a similar situation, I thought, but not to Adam who had worked with Ben and me from the beginning and ought to have known better. 'You be fair with us and we'll be fair with you.' 'We want our boys to enjoy their working experience with us.' – these words and others had been repeated to Adam a thousand times – and recently in London when the oustings of Shirak and Karbi had been explained, as examples of the rule and not exceptions.

Failing to appreciate how we wished to conduct ourselves, and admitting that there had been nothing to indicate that our intentions had not been as we had professed, the past as a guide to the future was no comfort to him. Therefore the question of his liquidation (which was no academic exercise but a matter of life and death) had to be debated in terms of what we as intelligent but wholly unscrupulous people might consider to be the most expedient for ourselves, bearing in mind the present circumstances.

Unfortunately, as Adam was the first to point out, present circumstances amply illustrated his own argument. On the one hand he had insisted on complete anonymity and the utmost secrecy being preserved on his role and and whereabouts (thoroughly commendable from a security angle).

On the other hand he now twisted these very same arguments and requirements to illustrate his theory of the cunning of a plot which had ensured that no one knew where he was or even that he had left England, simply so that he could be more easily disposed of – *and without trace!*

'So, what you are suggesting is, that if you are not caught on the job you will be annihilated. In other words, you're a gonner anyway?'

'It seems bloody likely.'

'Why?'

'You would feel safer afterwards.'

'Ah! The epitaph on your grave: HE KNEW TOO MUCH. Is that what you mean? Utterly ludicrous. Have you thought what questions Paul would ask? Or Ben? Or for that matter Tania? – wonder whatever happened to old Adam?'

'I'm sure you'd find answers.'

'Probably could. But if we were prepared to resort to such methods we'd hardly be in the gold business, we'd be pushing drugs. We'd be in a business making ourselves hundreds of per cent profit per trip, offering carriers a few thousand instead of hundreds, then bumping them off to save ourselves the cost and at the same time eliminating a source of information that could bring us twenty years.'

'Well, why not in this instance?'

'Because it's simply not the way we wish to work, and you should know it. If it was, why have we not eliminated Shirak? It would save us hundreds of thousand of pounds a year – or more. It would be easy to send someone over from Hong Kong – and even dispose of *him* afterwards.

'Perhaps that's what you intend to do.'

There was no arguing!

'I'll have to accept your word,' he said, after several assurances.

'But you'll never be entirely convinced.'

After I had left a note for Phillip and Tania to say that I would be a further hour, we moved elsewhere for dinner, finding ourselves in a dim candlelit corner of a cafe south of the river, with strains of Mozart playing severely in the background. He had further complications to introduce.

He wanted his bird flown out, a girl he had known for scarcely two weeks. 'Cannot a half-starved idiot,' I thought, 'who has never made more than a few quid on his own initiative, control himself for such a short time to make the five grand for which he has been squealing all his life?'

'For obvious security reasons, it's totally out of the question. You must be out of your mind.'

'Five thousand pounds is not enough,' he said.

'It's enough. But whether it's enough or not is now beside the point. A deal is a deal.'

'I should have more. I want more.'

'Steady on. Now you're treading on dangerous ground. If you think you're in a bargaining position, you're wrong. If you are assuming that it is too late to find anybody else to do the job you're wrong. If you're imagining that you can capitalise on the weaknesses of your present condition, you're wrong. I'm not going to be squeezed by you. Nor blackmailed. You want to make a match of it? I'll cancel the operation altogether.'

'Blackmailed?'

'Yes, as far as I'm concerned, blackmailed. And do I have to remind you of what I've already said? 'You be fair with us and we'll be perfectly fair with you.' If you're not, then you will discover the cost. I'm warning you. London was where you should have persisted in your bargaining – at the time when I put the proposition to you. Not now. You had the possibility of accepting or rejecting the offer. You accepted. That's it.'

'You're going straight out to Hong Kong after the event?' I checked, after the subject of money had been dropped. 'As already agreed,' I emphasised.

'I'm not sure. I may have to go back to London.'

'Well, you have a week in which to decide. I have to

arrange your undetected exit from here, as well as your ticket.'

Adam was seriously disturbed and his mind had not quietened during the course of our meeting. We returned to each topic again and again and each time he was agitated, expressing his fears and complexes and confusing every simple issue. If he was to survive and do the job he would have to be found the grounds for trust and infused with some spirit.

'Think seriously,' I said. 'None of the terms of our original agreement are going to be changed. Bearing in mind all you have said this evening, are you quite sure, now that I have given you absolutely free choice in the matter, that you wish to carry on? If not, you can quit, without complications, and can fly back to London tomorrow.'

'I'll carry on.'

'You're completely certain?'

'Yes.'

'The job is utterly simple. The only complications are those you create in your own mind. If you don't think that your mental condition is likely to improve, then I'm advising you to pack up now.'

'No. I'll be all right.'

He returned to his hotel.

Though Adam believed he had been given free choice for the second time, he had forgotten one thing. The first transfer from the Hang Seng to 'Mr John Brown', Hotel Trumpy, Zurich, though it had not yet arrived, had already been despatched. So, whether he had decided to continue or not, he was, though not too incriminatingly, already involved – or, as he might put it, *trapped*.

I rejoined the others, but there was no respite for them.

I had particularly wanted to avoid calling Ben from Zurich. In normal circumstances I would have waited until the following day and done so from Geneva or Lausanne. However, in view of Adam's delicate state, any further delay in the arrival of the money might flip his mind over and out for good.

Phillip drove me to the central post office. First I telephoned Paul to check that his money had arrived all right. It had. And he had telexed it back to Hong Kong. He had flu. Unable to find a first class hotel, he had found a room in a private house and would be able to stay there indefinitely. The bank manager had expressed surprise at his visitor's passport, a document he hadn't seen before, but gave no impression that he would be querying it.

I was put through to the Repulse Bay Hotel.

'Adam's money still hasn't arrived. It's probably on its way via a Swiss bank which is no use at all. In future can you get "Stevenson" to insist that it's transferred direct to the Bank of America.'

It was past midnight before we were able to leave Zurich. The others had expected to drive on to Geneva, an estimated four hours away. This would mean that we had been on the go for almost twenty-four hours since leaving Brussels. Coping with Adam had drained my last energies. Both Phillip and Tania were dead.

'Why don't we stop in Zurich?' Phillip suggested.

This, of course, was out of the question. Our names could not appear on any hotel register there. Instead, we drove out in search of some quiet nearby village. I already had the suspicion that I might have to return in the morning. Sisyphus in Hades had a task which was to push a stone up a hill: as soon as he left it alone or got to the top, it rolled down again. Building up Adam's confidence would be a task like this.

Unloading the car was like moving office.

'We'll be up at six,' I said to Phillip.

Before collapsing into bed I discussed Adam's condition with Tania.

'We're going back to Zurich,' I told Phillip as he repacked the car.

We whizzed towards the city, refreshed by the crispness and beauty of the mountains and countryside and the sharp but invigorating air.

Phillip went for a boat-ride on the lake. Tania waited in a nearby café, while I called Adam.

'I've a card from some Swiss bank saying that the money has arrived,' he said.

'Good. Are you going to collect?'

'I'd like to see you first,' he replied, sounding very much as if he had returned to his former condition.

As we walked along the street I realised that he was even worse. It was as if he was on the verge of an epileptic fit. The stone had rolled downhill.

We joined Tania, whose presence, I felt, would be most reassuring. Seated at a café near the Bahnhof he broke into convulsions – literally – and his whole body trembled. He was unable to speak. He collapsed into a shivering, blubbering mess.

We sat saying little. Tania, sweet and soothing, worked miracles. There was only one thing to do: to get him on the first plane out. But, before this, he had to collect the money.

'The bank manager,' he blubbered, 'has queried my passport.' He had forgotten to mention this the previous day. However, as with Paul, the manager had done no more than express his surprise at seeing it.

It was two hours before he felt at peace again. He apologised for his behaviour, volunteered to collect the money, did so, and subsequently handed it to me.

'All right,' I said. 'Why don't you think the whole matter over during the next few days. Go back to London for the weekend. I'll meet you there. However, just in case you consider returning, you should go first of all to the Bank of America and see the manager. Pay some money in and ask him for an explanation of why you had to collect from a Swiss bank when the transfer had been sent specifically to your account with him. Also, when you check out of your hotel, re-book for Thursday, saying that you are going to Lausanne for a few days. You can then travel out in your own name. Before I leave, I'll arrange for a telegram to be sent from Lausanne in the name of "Mr Brown" cancelling your reservation and re-booking elsewhere, then it can be established later on that whereas your own exit on this day balanced with your entrance a few days earlier, "Mr Brown" had remained in the country. Okay? Will that clear your mind of the problem?'

He left to book his flight. Tania, Phillip and myself drove west; to Lausanne, where I put a call through to Ben; to Geneva – whose mood was flamboyantly summerish – where we would be based.

Chapter 15/London: 'Mr. X'

There was no such person as 'Mr X' but in the process of detailing my plans it became necessary to postulate his existence. He became the miracle man used to solve unsolved equations, and had the amazing attribute of being able to appear in several places several hundreds of kilometres apart at almost the same time.

My plan for the crucial days had only been partially formulated. On both Friday 2nd and Monday 5th August, some three weeks off, Paul in Amsterdam and Adam in Zurich would enter branches of the Bank of America and simultaneously draw separate amounts of $150,000, totally $600,000. Each of these amounts, *after* conversion in the case of Amsterdam and *before* conversion in the case of Zurich, had to be taken four hours journey away: from Amsterdam in Holland to 'X' in Brussels, Belgium; from Zurich to Phillip in Geneva. Though Zurich was the centre of the gold market in Switzerland, and though Amsterdam had recently opened its gold market for the first time since 1940 and was the centre of diamond buying in Europe, neither our carriers nor any acting station manager could be permitted to go there; nor should they know that we had any dealings there. They would know only the links London-Brussels-Hong Kong and London-Geneva-Hong Kong. Any exception would have to be trusted as much as the two collectors.

The decision posed problems.

How would the two sums collected by Adam be brought to Geneva? It was out of the question that Adam himself delivered to Phillip: firstly because Phillip had no knowledge of Adam's presence in Switzerland (believing him to be in the North of England): secondly because Phillip had to be made to believe that the money he received came from

146/How to Rob Banks Without Violence

Brussels or London as part of the large loan which he had already been informed we had raised in the Far East. There was another problem: if Phillip received $150,000 on the Friday and then read in the papers that *the same amount* had been whipped from a bank in Zurich *on the same day*, he might well become suspicious. So, though it was doubtful anyway whether the money could be delivered to him in time to make his gold purchases on Friday, it was better held over the week-end; and somebody would have to be found, both to hold it and to act as intermediary.

Both tasks were allocated to Mr X.

But did Mr X have to be yet another person introduced? Why couldn't I perform the tasks myself? Because I would almost certainly be running the shuttle service from Amsterdam. At any rate I had to allow myself the maximum freedom. Then why not Tania? Why not? Though it was bad policy to use a bird in such an operation, she was not any old bird. She had proved herself well-briefed, thoroughly reliable and absolutely discreet; besides which we were engaged to be married.

In this instance the need for a Mr X vanished; but, as other unresolved details emerged, he reappeared quickly.

Adam had insisted that he be paid in Zurich immediately after his second withdrawal. As he could obviously not be paid in the traceable notes from the bank (and our spare capital was earmarked for the fares of twenty carriers) some of the gold which Phillip bought on the Monday would have to be converted (back into cash) – a job that could not be done by Phillip, who might again become suspicious.

This was a job for Mr X. Tania could not do it because she would have left Geneva for Zurich at 7.30 in the morning. Even if both tasks could theoretically be performed by the same person, X could not be informed of the fraud. Later in the day he too would have to go to Zurich and hand Adam his fee. While he was there, he could deliver Adam across the Swiss-German border. Why couldn't Adam go out under his own steam? Because his own name should not be allowed to appear on any records (as it might do if he left by 'plane, train or hired car), and as 'Brown' he should seem to have vanished into thin air.

Mr X had become less a convenient abstraction and more a person who would have to be found in the flesh. As his activities would cause him to be suspicious, he would have to be someone with a vested interest in keeping his mouth shut. Only one person fitted the bill: one of our investors, a property speculator called Hamish. The fact that he was a great friend of Adam's would be of great assurance to Adam when it came to delivering his fee and escorting him out of the country. I would approach him during my forced visit to London.

I left Geneva, sunlight sparkling on the lake and shimmering over the not too distant snow-topped peaks. Tania had been despatched to Lausanne to cable Mr Brown's hotel. Phillip was to plot the flights of carriers at the rate of two a day from the fifth onwards. Sinking through dense cloud and fog we landed at Heathrow. I called Adam and met him at a restaurant, which was conveniently empty.

'Are you sure the idea can work?'

'Yes it can and will,' I said. 'It's utterly simple.'

Once again I went over every detail. I assured him of his fee and safety and spoke of his future in the organisation. He had pulled himself together remarkably well. Too well, I thought.

'I want an extra five thousand pounds,' he said.

'All right,' I said, after prolonged argument. 'You'll be paid the first immediately you've done the job and the second immediately on your arrival in Hong Kong – provided you're out there within four days.'

I had no intention of honouring other than our original agreement.

After extensive argument it was agreed that his bird could visit him in Zurich. 'Okay,' I said, 'but she is never to visit your hotel. She is not even to be allowed to know where you are staying or what name you're using. Nor are you ever to telephone her from your hotel. And she is to be back in England at the time of the event – and be left with the impression that you've gone to Italy. Is that agreed?'

But she couldn't be there for another ten days. Meanwhile he would be lonely and could he visit us in Geneva?

'You realise that you will not be able to register into a hotel?' I asked. 'Where are you going to sleep? In the woods?'

'In the car.'

'Suppose you are found and questioned? Assumed drunk? And you have no licence. The whole operation could be loused up. Do you realise that Phillip would know of your presence in Switzerland? And that such a breach of agreed procedure would involve a great deal of cover-up work on my part? And don't you consider that it would be dangerous in the future, with Phillip in possession of this knowledge?'

As joint head of what might be seen by the eyes of the law as a criminal organisation, and as organiser of this operation, I should have been commanding him to perform and imposing the agreed terms, with threats of violence. Failing to obey and proving too tedious then he *should* have been eliminated, as simply discharging him would have been too risky. Instead, the sufferer of incalculable anxiety and complications, I had no choice but to make concessions – not only because he held the trump card at this time (it was too late to replace him) but because some of these concessions were necessary to prevent the balance of his mind being disturbed again. His chances of survival if left alone in Zurich were minimal.

With new conditions agreed to, he went on to discuss the practical details. He was instructed on the handover:

'Go to the Swissair Terminal underneath the station. It has an entrance of its own on the bridge side. Tania will be there from a few minutes after 11.30 a.m. onwards. Don't say anything to her or show any recognition. You will arrive there with a Swissair bag – so you'd better purchase one the day before. Casually go and seat yourself next to her and place your bag next to hers, which will be identical. While seated, be thumbing through an air time-table, then go and make some enquiries about a ticket. Tania will make the switch. On Monday do the same thing. Just make sure, on both occasions, that any wrapping around the wads has been removed first.

'Hamish will arrive with your fee at about four in the afternoon. Then he will drive you into Germany. Are these arrangements satisfactory?'

'Yes.'

'Have you no complications to add?' I asked sarcastically.

'Well, if I'm going to be done up, I'm going to be done up anyway.'

'Very philosophical of you! By the way, do you think that Hamish *will* be prepared to offer his services?'

'Yes, I'm sure.'

'Just tell him that his presence is required urgently by both of us for one week. Say nothing else. I'll break his roles to him casually as I go along.'

Chapter 16/Geneva: From Alpha to Omega

'So that your entry into Switzerland will be entirely untraceable this time, I'll arrange for you to be picked up by car at Ostend,' I said to Adam, not realising what a mammoth performance this would prove to be.

We left the restaurant. I went to a phone box, dialled the club, put on a moody voice and asked for Shirak. He was out, so I decided to put in a diplomatic appearance.

'How's Tania?' asked henchman-in-chief Belman, who had insisted that I wait and had called Shirak unsuccessfully at every game in town.

'Fine. She's in Ireland. I'm just over here for a couple of days and going back tomorrow.'

I took a cab to the West End to call Ben. This tedious discipline of going frequently miles out of the way and sitting about for hours in drab places in order to ensure that our communications were untraceable would pay off handsomely in the future, I had thought. It was 4.00 a.m. before I was in bed.

In the morning I brought Adam and Robert Wyndham together to check suits and rehearse the procedures for despatching the carriers, before returning to the West End to call Paul.

The transfers of money had been going smoothly. In fact everything in Amsterdam had been going smoothly. With one exception:

'The quantity of 1½ carat diamonds which we require is unobtainable,' Paul said.

'How much is obtainable?' I asked.

'Only about $60,000 worth.'

'That's odd,' I said, considering Amsterdam's position

as European diamond centre. 'How come the supply is so short?'

'I don't know, but I'm going to Antwerp on Monday to have a look there. I'm being taken by one of the main dealers here.'

'Excellent!' If Adam was like Paul, the operation would be a walkover.

'Shall I order larger ones?'

'No. Only what I've told you. We know we can sell these. We'll just have to buy more gold with the difference.'

'I can take a load on the way out, if you like.'

Such enthusiasm!

Early afternoon I met Hamish. Late afternoon I was in Geneva.

Not wishing to be the heartless shatterer of the pleasantly shaping scenes that Tania and Phillip had found for themselves in my absence I broke the news gently that we would be rising at five and going on a long journey north. Phillip was required to drive, but though Tania had the choice it seemed that however dull or tedious a venture promised to be she was not going to be left out – even though it was pointed out to her that we would not be stopping at our destination but coming straight back. This intention I could not convey to Phillip without the explanation that I wished to avoid all record of the journey, as he would consider it utterly ludicrous.

We dined early, soaked ourselves in Yugoslavian Riesling, returned to our separate studio suites and slept.

Avoiding the way through France and Luxembourg, which would have been quicker and more picturesque but which might have involved paper formalities at the French frontiers, we took the familiar route through Lausanne, Berne, Zurich, Basle and up through Germany. We hit Brussels at about nine, meeting torrential rain as we approached the country's sole autobahn and reached Ostend, seaport and relic playground of Victoriana, sixteen hours after our dawn departure. Six hours later, battered and blinded by a blizzard which made our vehicle seem less like a car than a bathyscope, Adam's intrepid driving had brought us back close to the German border. At this point Phillip, the only one with a licence, took over; he had been roused from his kip in the back where he had also been serving a very useful function as a warm pillow for Tania. Thereafter I took the wheel myself. The vehicle now became less of a bathyscope but a knife which cut through the night. We met dawn not with the expected sonic bang but a disappointing whimper as Riviera bound traffic brought us to a succession of halts.

Arriving in Zurich we dropped Adam who gave us an unconvincing imitation of a cheerful grin, and continued westward. We had now been on the go for thirty-six hours and the resultant drowsiness and exhaustion were almost overwhelming, but the end was not yet. At Berne we stopped for an hour while I telephoned Ben. Had the last transfer arrived from Paul in Amsterdam? Had it been sent off to Zurich? And had 'Stevenson' insisted and been assured of the fact that it would pass directly from the Hang Seng to the Bank of America this time? If we passed through Lausanne, I did not notice. Last reserves of energy had fought all out and lost. At the Rue des Alpes I was rudely awoken. We staggered upstairs and slumped into happy heapdom.

Having spent the last six days moving like a creature on hot bricks – London, Amsterdam, Brussels, Zurich, back to Zurich, Lausanne, Geneva, London, Geneva, Ostend, Zurich, Berne and back to Geneva – much of the days following was spent relaxing. We dined with friends, went for picnics in the mountains and knife-throwing in the woods, browsed around Lausanne, crossed into France to spend an evening at Divonne and the casino, drove through the seven mile tunnel of Mont Blanc into Italy, climbed to the foot of the Valleé Blanche glacier and took a cable-car up the jagged perpendicular face of the Aiguille du Midi from quiet sunlight to overhanging ice, mist and howling Arctic-like winds.

The transfers continued. In Zurich we visited Adam who had once again decided to pack it in.

'Okay,' I said, not intending to make the smallest argument. 'Return to London. Forget the whole thing. I don't mind one bit. Frankly I've had enough.'

This response surprised him enormously. He changed his mind rapidly: but he was still worried. The bank manager had again queried his passport and Adam was convinced that he was going to make enquiries with some British authority. Despite his howling I considered things in Zurich, as in Amsterdam, in perfect order. But I had yet to finalise the overall plan.

Phase One of the operation, consisting of placing the key men, Paul, Adam, Phillip and Robert Wyndham, in their respective positions, Amsterdam, Zurich, Geneva, and London, briefing and organising them in their jobs, was complete.

Phase Two consisted of the collection of Friday's and Monday's withdrawals from Paul (less what was necessary for his diamond purchases), the conversion into gold in Amsterdam, the transport of this gold to Brussels, the collection of Friday's and Monday's withdrawals from Adam, the deliveries to Phillip in Geneva for conversion into gold, the exits of the two collectors, the despatch of carriers from London to Brussels and Geneva to pick up the gold and fly it to Hong Kong; and clearing out from Geneva.

I had detailed the sequence of events in Switzerland as follows:

FRIDAY (2nd August):

Tania catches a train leaving *Geneva* at 7.30 a.m., waits at the Swissair terminal from 11.30 a.m. onwards, and collects from Adam.

SATURDAY:

A clear day. *Tania* holds the money in Geneva.

SUNDAY:

Instructions on the rotation of carriers having been given to *Robert Wyndham*, liaison having been established between *Wyndham* and Phillip, and accommodation booked, *Wyndham* despatches two carriers from *London* to *Geneva*. In the evening *Tania* hands the money to Phillip.

MONDAY:

Tania repeats her Friday journey and collects *Adam's* second withdrawal from the bank, returns to *Geneva* and hands part of it to Phillip the same evening.

Phillip buys seventy-two kilos of gold at one bank and arranges transport to another bank for safe-keeping. He will need an *assistant*. He loads two carriers and takes them to the airport for their separate flights to Hong Kong.

Phillip, having bought the gold, will have to give £5,000 worth ($12,000) to 'Mr X' (*assuming* the co-operation of Hamish). 'Mr X' sells this gold at a third bank then drives to *Zurich* to pay *Adam* and drop him across the border in Germany.

Phillip will meet another two incoming carriers from *London*, for despatch on Tuesday morning.

There were other details. Phillip, after he had despatched the last of the carriers, would himself fly to Hong Kong. Who would return his hired car to England? What would happen to the reserve carriers' suits in Phillip's possession? What would happen to Tania and our considerable luggage? Should she fly direct to Hong Kong to await me there at the Mandarin, and if so would she be able to negotiate my locked black boxes and confidential papers through customs? No. She would have to be brought from Geneva to wherever I would be. By whom?

The plan for *Amsterdam* was still in embryo. The resolved and unresolved details stood as follows: much depended on the amount of diamonds that Paul would be able to purchase. So far he had been able to reserve no more than $60,000. This left $240,000 to be converted into gold. A quick calculation showed that eight carriers would be required. As all of them would be picking up their loads in Brussels, a police check on Amsterdam – Far East flights would show nothing. Two questions had to be answered: Who would do the buying in Amsterdam? And who would do the transporting to Brussels?

Whoever did the purchasing would need an assistant. Paul could be excluded as he would be dealing with diamond merchants after which he would leave the city independently. Transport would be needed. Could not 'Mr X' be employed before being sent down to Geneva? Even if he could, another was still required. Peter – who had been lined up as a reserve on my return from the Far East? And even if 'X' could be used on the Friday, who would replace him on the Monday?

Even more important: who would collect from Paul?

Unfortunately I would not be able to visit Paul before the 2nd for any final briefing; the demands of Adam were still seeing to that. But I could meet him on D-Day itself immediately after he had been to the bank. I could base myself in Brussels, arriving there the previous day from London, leave Brussels at about seven on the Friday, driven by 'X' and accompanied by Peter, meet Paul, hand the money to 'X' with instructions to buy gold, and leave its transportation to both him and Peter. Before leaving Brussels I would convince 'X' that I already had the money for the purchase with me.

These details were tentative and took no account of the Monday, but I had time, though precious little of it, to elaborate on them.

On reconsidering the theory of the fraud itself I was certain that there was no flaw in it. And I was particularly certain of the unique fact that we had ten clear days after the withdrawals had been made before any fraud could be discovered – *provided that* there was nothing in the behaviour of the collectors that caused suspicion.

Daniel Grant had assured us of this. And would he, with six years of brooding on the idea while working in the transfer department of his own head office, have risked his career, in the prominent position, plus his last $10,000 while uncertain on this and other vital points? But this question didn't really have to be answered, because not only had his own explanations and assurances made sense but they had fitted in with what I had seen written in black and white in his bank's confidential internal procedure sheets.

Despite the certainties it was impossible to ignore the possibilities of a total or partial collapse. Failure at the time of withdrawal could still occur. But even this could not be disastrous. Payment might be delayed, but no on-the-spot check could be made on the authenticity of the cable. If the collector felt that payment had been delayed because he was suspected then he had time to get away and only the project in that place would be abandoned. A blow-out in one place could not possibly affect another. By the time that the banks had learnt of a second attempt, the money would already have been drawn out. So even with the possibility of failure we still had two irons in the fire. The odds against failure in both places were long. If the worst came to the worst we stood to make a minimum of $150,000.

However, not without consequences.

How would either of the collectors react if they were caught?

'Remember,' I told them both, 'if ever you get caught and get more than two years, we'll get you out, even if it costs us most of our capital and means mounting an operation bigger than this. It'll be good g's. And don't worry, you'll be looked after and your future will be taken care of.'

Despite such assurances, infinitely more effective than threats, there was still the possibility that either would break or betray himself – or even, it was impossible to tell, maliciously betray others. As much time had to be put into considering the consequences of any of these eventualities and precautionary counter-moves as into the plan itself.

'Will any traces of possible dangerous consequences be left behind?' This was a question which had to be answered before any communication or transfer of money could be made to anyone anywhere – and similarly in connection with presences and movement of personnel. Fingerprints left behind by the two collectors would be of no consequence as neither had any form and I would make it my business to ensure that this remained so in the future.

In the event of a threat of total collapse after successful withdrawals, with Bank of America trufflehounds hot on some trail, there were several interesting possibilities. Sitting on the codes along with other even more valuable material, and with or without the knowledge of our source of supply, were we not in a position to squeeze them by the bollocks to our hearts contents and without their having the means to protect themselves? And were we not in an excellent bargaining position?

'We have limited our interest to $600,000. We have no interest in doing anything further. You may change your codes, but we will have the same access to these as to the present ones. Aside from the codes we have supplies of all of your documents of transfer, copies of your own internal procedures on their usage, specimen signatures of managers and cashiers of every branch of yours in every country of the world. Can you suspend all banking operations and change all these? You can arrest me, that is if you can present adequate proof, but how will you stop the contingency strike plans which my organisation has ready to put immediately into effect. You release our man, drop all further investigations, and I'll guarantee that we'll refrain from making any use, directly or indirectly, of any material we have.'

This would be no bluff as they would be provided with evidence of what we had. If some might consider these ideas to be ridiculously far-fetched, I considered them utterly realistic. So long as I was not caught on the spot myself, and survived a couple of weeks, I would have ample time to prepare for exactly such a contingency. It might not even be necessary to wait for them to come to us; perhaps our positions would be better protected if we approached them even before the fraud was detected.

Aside from these thoughts of possible collapses and the foolproofing of our positions, there was the immediate after-event situation to be planned. Around twenty carriers would be arriving in Hong Kong, a dozen of whom would be remaining. Accommodation as well as cover jobs would have to be found for them. I had worked out the principles of a training programme, which I would begin to put into effect as soon as I arrived and the object of which was to make them into a useful and reliable working force, capable of holding responsible posts, that would be used in building up an empire of separate smuggling operations throughout the Far East, while simultaneously engaging in the legitimate commercial business Ben and I already had in mind.

Chapter 17/London: Pure Fantasy

The day was Friday 27th July. There were seven to go. I left Tania and Phillip in Geneva and flew to London.

I had arranged to meet Karbi on the Sunday, the day he was due to return from Norway, but learnt soon after arrival that he was already in London. Wishing to put off seeing him for as long as possible, as he would not leave me out of his sight, I was fortunate in finding circumstances through which I would be able to demonstrate my attempts to get hold of him and explain my failure.

I booked into a hotel, leaving a suitcase full of clothes there, so that when we were finally in contact he would be less likely to discover that I had not after all given up my flat in Courtfield Gardens.

After this I made routine calls from Trafalgar Square. Paul reported that $60,000 worth of diamonds had already been selected and sealed and Adam seemed reasonably contented in Zurich. The final telexes had already come through and the capital transferred elsewhere. Ben was not available.

Late evening, unable to find a cab, I walked up Cromwell Road on my way back to try Ben again. The streets were empty. Who should enter my vision, standing at a corner on the opposite side of the road, also looking for a taxi it seemed, but Karbi. Evasion was impossible. Spotting me he yelled. We met like long lost brothers.

'Karbi, where have you been?' I asked, as if it were a great riddle to me, 'I rang you this morning in Norway. Your number's been changed and when I finally tracked you down your wife simply said that you were out. When did you arrive?'

'A week ago.'

'Where are you going now?'

'I was just going to the club. Where were you going?'

'Just up to the Whisky,' I said, desperately trying to think how I could shake him off and put my call through.

'Come to the club.'

'No. I don't want to get involved with Shirak. You know how I feel about the subject. No contact. He gets his money – that's all. Seeing him will mean discussing business. It will be embarrassing having to avoid the subject. The less he knows the better for all.'

'You don't have to discuss business. He just wants to see you. He's extremely fond of you.'

'We'll meet for lunch tomorrow,' I suggested as we walked. 'Everything's in order. I've been to Hatton Garden and organised the diamond merchants. I've selected the stones and they're now sealed and ready for collection. You want to come and see them?'

This was a safe question, as he had shown earlier that he did not want his face to be seen within a mile of them.

'The man is ready to collect from the bank. He has his passport. That cost me two hundred pounds, twice what I expected, but it's a good job. There are still problems though. We have to discuss the details of his handover to us. One serious danger, is that he might organise his mates for a hijack.'

'Is that likely?'

'No. But so long as it's theoretically possible, we have to consider it. The delivery plan must be foolproof. Where is he going to deliver to us? How, and to whom? I personally don't want to touch the money – not, at least, directly from him, or on the same day.'

'I'll do it,' he stated, rather over-eagerly.

'That would be unwise,' I said. 'He should never know who you are, or even be able to recognise you. I intend to be out in the country during the day myself.'

I brought the subject to a quick close and we concentrated on finding a taxi. He had made up his mind to accompany me to the Whisky at all costs and there was nothing I could do. Rather than let me out of his sight, he would follow me to a party in the sewers. It was two hours before I was finally able to escape, and even then by disappearing from the club when his back was turned.

The next day I waited half an hour for him – before deciding that his lateness was a perfect opportunity for another evasion – and left. Then to show my good intentions I telephoned Shirak.

'Where the hell's your damn brother? He's pissing around,' I said. 'He was supposed to see me for lunch.'

'I'll give him hell,' Shirak assured me after a more detailed explanation.

I left him to do so, happy to have some extra time to complete the details of the fantasy fraud and attend to other details of the real one.

The next day I was sitting in the basement of Lyon's in Knightsbridge. Opposite me was an eager Karbi. I was so nervous that my stomach muscles had tightened up so much that eating was impossible.

'The deal takes place a week from today. The money will arrive about midday,' I said. 'Well, to be accurate, it will be there as soon as the bank opens in the morning; but I have told our man to present himself at midday. Everything is in order.'

I went on to explain exactly what was in order, still without naming any bank. He understood that the source of the money was not legitimate, but that the transfer itself was.

'No,' I repeated, 'I can't disclose the names of the people with whom we are dealing. Ben and I have assured them that none other than ourselves should know of any of the details. We intend keeping our agreement. It works both ways. If anything goes wrong, you don't know their names; they don't know yours. You know nothing of the theory of the operation, therefore you are without clues which

F

might assist others to find out who is responsible. All are protected.'

This argument covered a vast range of difficult questions. 'Don't worry about the theory,' I said, 'it's all perfectly sound. You trust my intelligence in the matter?'

'Oh yes. Completely.'

'There's only one thing that we have to worry about and that is making the collection and converting the proceeds without leaving any tracks.'

'What's the problem of delivery by your man?'

'Well, two things. The first: I won't take delivery from him myself.'

A reasonable demonstration of the fact that I was not too anxious to get my hands on the money, I thought.

'Secondly: I trust my man completely and would bet a million on the fact that he will deliver. He's got a wife and kids to whom he's fondly attached. I know his whole scene inside out, from his mates to his brand of toothbrush. He won't run; but the point is this: Though I'm certain he'll follow to the letter every detail of the instructions I give him, to demonstrate his prima facie straightness, from any point after he has made his delivery he can arrange a hijack. He's got mates – and mates with form. And I wouldn't put it past him. Even if I had no doubt, we should still protect ourselves against the unlikely. But first: who can he deliver to?'

'Why not you?'

'If any crunch comes, I don't want any finger pointing in my direction. I'd rather be well out of the way; What ideas do you have?'

'Supposing he delivers to me?'

'Then he'll remember your face.'

'So? He won't see it again or be able to put a name to it.'

'Okay. However, count on the fact that he will remember it. And don't forget the obvious London–Hong Kong link. Not-too-penetrating enquiries afterwards are going to discover, thanks entirely to your brother, that two Sher-kasians have been running a gold smuggling business. Get the picture? That fact unearthed and his remembrance of your face and 'Click!'. It's your decision if you want to expose yourself to this risk.'

'Yeah. You're right.'

'Anyway. Assuming an attempted hijack, will one person be enough? With three-hundred-and-fifty thousand dollars in the suitcase – one clonk on the head and that's that. Dead easy. And why not? The question is: can he arrange one with impunity? The answer is, as I've already said: so long as his own contract can be seen to be fulfilled, that is, while he remains in possession and right up until the handover. Any damage after that – well, we'd be in no position to prove anything. What could we do? Bump him off on a hunch, when he will be able to argue reasonably that he has done his job and that what has happened must be on account of some leak in our own organisation? You see, we must imagine the worst *now* and take every precaution. What would you do in his position?'

We considered numerous possibilities and Karbi became more and more involved.

'Have you told him where or when the deal will take place?' he asked.

'Not yet. I've arranged to see him on Thursday. He'll be on standby from Sunday onwards.'

On Thursday, I would be on the boat to Ostend.

'Where do you suggest a hand-over takes place?' he asked.

'Anywhere where his case can be left securely, where it can be watched from that time on, and collected when the coast is seen to be clear.'

'A station?'

'No.'

I had already worked out what I considered to be the best arrangement in these imaginary circumstances, but the more he exercised his own imagination and felt a sense of participation the better. I allowed him to hold the floor for as long as he was able.

'What about a telephone kiosk?' he asked.

'That's it!' I said, having completed the diagram which would illustrate my own proposal.

'There are two on the corner of the street on the opposite side of the Cromwell Road from Shirak's flat. What about those? He's on the third floor, isn't he? You'll have to check that the trees in front don't block the view If they don't, anybody in the flat will be able to see both kiosks quite clearly and all approaches to them.'

He began to draw his own diagram.

'Now, my man will not be told that this is the delivery place. In fact he will be made to believe it is quite definitely not. I'll simply send him to the kiosk for his delivery instructions. Let us say that he is to be there at the latest at nine-thirty in the evening. At ten o'clock he will hear the telephone in one of the kiosks ring. He will answer it and do precisely what he's told.'

'And I,' said Karbi, 'will be able to see whether he has been followed or not. Tell him to park in front of the kiosk.'

'No,' I replied. 'If I do that, he'll know he's going to be watched and figure that it must be the delivery place. I'll tell him that he'll be using his car and that it must have a full tank as the delivery is outside London. It will be after this telephone call that he'll plan to pass on the information about where he's going.

'If you see that he has been followed or think he might have been or just want to put the fear of God into him then all you have to do is a little bluff. Come to think of it, it might be a good idea anyway. It would certainly make him think twice before double-crossing us.'

'How?' Karbi was on the edge of his seat.

'When he picks up the phone, you give your name, let's say Augustus. 'Okay,' you say. 'Now, first I want you to move your head to the left and keep it facing in that direction.

Keep it there as long as you like, then move it back again. I will tell you precisely when you have done so.' This done, you give him shock number two: 'There is a rifle with telescopic sights and a silencer pointing straight at you. Don't put your hands up. Don't move.' Right, after this there are numerous possibilities. But, get the picture? You can say, 'You were followed to this kiosk, and move on from there, or, if he was not, then carry on with your hand-over instructions.'

'I think I'll use Belman,' he interrupted. 'He need know nothing.'

'Okay, that's fine.'

'Also, I'll use a Beretta. I have one in the hotel.'

Bluff, I suspected, although he had previously convinced me that he would not hesitate to use one. There was not a neutron of suspicion on his face. He had believed everything I'd said.

'When you have seen that the streets are empty and that everything is okay, you tell him to stroll southwards and keep walking straight, even, you say, if he has to walk half a mile. He walks until another gentleman approaches him . . . '

And so, we talked without a break for the next five or six hours, except for a quick change of surroundings from the cafeteria to the Hyde Park Hotel, working out, checking and re-checking, all the details. I would not be on the scene that day. Two days later, Karbi would hand me the cash, I would make the diamond purchases, and together we would fly off to Hong Kong. He, Ben and myself would set up a new organisation into which he would bring three of his American and Canadian friends. I listened to several old tunes – 'Together we will be unconquerable,' and, 'You will only have to say whatever you want of me, R.K., and I will do it'. He moaned on for at least half an hour in this vein and every minute saw him more excited. Then suddenly he stopped talking and stared at me. His face was very flushed.

'We must be brothers,' he pronounced; 'We must be friends and brothers forever.' I nodded politely and he tore the gold signet ring from his finger and thrust it at me.

'Wear this. Wear it always.'

'I can't. It's yours.'

'We are brothers. It's yours now. Wear it. I insist.'

I slipped it on a finger. 'Thank you,' I muttered, overcome. Karbi gave one last passionate stare, then pushed his face into his hands and wept. A magnificent coup de théâtre. How could I ever betray such affection – such trust?

Ex-beachboy Peter, who had been lured from his usual season of chat and chase by the prospects of gold-smuggling, was now on board, ensconced on a very hard seat and slouched over a table cursing the god-unearthly hour and endeavouring to kip. It was Thursday 1st August. We had left London at three in the morning and were now steaming across the Channel to Ostend. 'X', now Hamish, feeling boredom more than discomfiture, decided to drop traditional reserve, to reveal some rather dodgy spots on his otherwise impeccable city-gent-type front, and air one or two very un-city-type propositions:

'What do you think about organising a coup d'état in the Dominican Republic?' he asked out of the blue but with obvious seriousness. 'It's quite feasible. It could be done with one plane, one boat and about a hundred and fifty men,' he went on.

I checked the codes for the last time – a thoroughly useless activity as it was too late to make any adjustments at this point. I checked the distribution of our finance. Ben would be low in funds in Hong Kong, I thought, if our Korean customer's transfer had not yet arrived from New York. I attempted to think of small details I might have overlooked. The boat stank.

We drove to Brussels.

'Okay, Peter, I'll pick you up at six in the morning,' I said as we dropped him at his hotel. The expression on his face suggested that he had not been enormously impressed by the supposed glamour of his new profession. 'Be outside, wearing your "suit".'

Hamish and I went to the Hilton. There I deposited three grand in sterling in a safe-deposit box, the management retaining one key while I held the other, and moved into a double room in anticipation of Tania, whose arrival from Geneva after she had collected Monday's withdrawal was one of the small details that had so far not been worked out. I took a cab to the Gare du Midi to call Adam. I felt there was no need to call Paul and as agreed I would not contact Ben until I was able to report a victory.

'There wouldn't be much blood,' Hamish murmured, as we parted after dinner. We were obviously miles apart.

I collapsed into bed.

D Day, Friday

Only when we were on our way was Peter informed that our destination was Amsterdam. He would be briefed later. He sat in the front, with Hamish at the wheel, while I was spread out in the rear. My black case, along with myself, had been stripped of all papers relating to the gold business and the current operation. Being exceptionally strong it would be used for transporting the gold, though not more than twelve kilo bars could be carried inconspicuously by one arm. We had an estimated four hours' driving ahead, north via Antwerp.

In Hong Kong Ben would now be preparing to send his assistant 'Mr John Stevenson' to the Central Post Office to despatch the first two cables. Thereafter he would be in his hotel room, where he had sworn he would remain, without a bird, until contacted. Not only did he have no means of contacting me, but for all he knew, I might have been in Baghdad. In Zurich, 'Mr John Brown', undoubtedly in the throws of a trauma, would be counting the seconds, though several hours remained, before he entered the bank. In Geneva, Tania would be catching her train to Zurich for her Swissair Terminal rendezvous. Phillip would be out for the count in his studio without an inkling of what was going on. In London, Robert Wyndham would be waiting around the clock with two carriers ready to be sent to wherever instructed at a moment's notice. In Amsterdam, 'Mr

John Nicholas Robinson' would be waiting for me at midday at the Pop Bar in the Rembrandtplein, after he had been to the bank and before making his diamond purchases. In Korea, Daniel Grant would be holding himself at the Bank of America in agitated uncertainty. Two days previously, unknown to myself, he had sent a cable to Ben, via New York through the U.S. forces communications network, which read, 'SORRY TO HEAR RECENT DEATH OF YOUR MOTHER'. A warning of some sort?

Arriving in Amsterdam, we went straight to the Rembrandtplein, parked and sat in the Pop Bar. It was scruffy and the worst possible place for a rendezvous – stinking of conspiracy and down and outs. We had arrived early. To get Peter out of the way I sent him on a boat trip around the canals, telling him to be back at two o'clock. Hamish and I moved to a restaurant next door, from which I had an excellent view of passers-by – and he of the interior. Neither knew that I had a meeting.

By now the cable would have arrived at the bank and been decoded. Should there be any delay in paying out, Paul had been instructed to put on pressure. He could do so confidently, knowing that they had no means of on-the-spot verification. 'A timid approach will be more prone to suspicion than an aggressive one,' I had said. 'Anyway, be polite.' Though he would never have inspired anyone with the brains in his head, his appearance and manners were excellent. Also, he had always shown admirable coolness in situations which were potentially hot.

In the middle of lunch I saw him approaching and apologised to Hamish, exclaiming that I had just spotted a girl-friend and was going to leave for a few minutes chat.

Paul was on edge – the first time I had ever seen him so. 'How did it go?' I asked, as we sat in the bar.

'It didn't,' he replied.

'What do you mean 'it didn't'? It arrived, didn't it?'

'Yes, but he wouldn't pay out.'

'Why not?'

'I'm worried,' he replied. 'He has sent a telegram.'

'Well, that's nothing to worry about. I can guarantee the codes are right and every detail of the cable is correct. If he sent a telegram it will only be to check with his own head office that the bank in Hong Kong has sufficient credit balances with them. Did he tell you where he'd sent the telegram?'

'Yes. San Francisco.'

'Well, that, if you remember, is where their head offices are. So you've nothing to worry about. It's exactly as I said. Which is exactly as our bank man told us. There's nothing out of order and nothing unusual in this. The head office will reply by cablegram saying, 'Yes. Hang Seng have sufficient balances with us'. Their reply will be back at the bank tomorrow and you will be able to collect first thing on Monday.'

'I had a row with him,' he said. 'I was rude to him. I'm afraid I overdid it.'

'After or before he told you he had sent the telegram?'

'After, I think.'

'Well, think again. You should be certain.'

'Yes, it was after. No, it was at the same time more or less. It was after he told me that there would be a delay before I could collect and I told him that I needed the money urgently to pay for diamonds which I'd already ordered and had to be shipped abroad this afternoon. Then, at the same time, he told me the reason for the delay. Yes, that was it. It was to check the balance at head office.'

'You see, we anticipated this delay. The best thing you can do is to go back to the bank – and, if you really think you have overdone your bit, indirectly straighten things out with him and recheck your position. If he did have reasons to be suspicious, then he would be playing the oldest trick in the book asking you to come back the next day – in this case, Monday. Also it would be the last thing he would expect you to do now.

'Go back and ask him how long the delay will be. Say to him that it makes no difference to you whether it is two or three days. Say that you are just on your way to see your diamond merchant to put off your deal, but that before doing so you want a date from the bank which you can rely on, the latest date at which the transfer will be cleared for payment as you don't want to have to make yet another postponement. At the same time, you can apologise for your anger this morning, which you can say was due to your incredible surprise along with the knowledge that you would be caused very considerable inconvenience.'

'I don't like it,' he said. 'I'm scared.'

'Well,' I said, 'only you can judge the personal situation between you and the bank manager. Relationships to date have been satisfactory, haven't they? Have you had any trouble with prompt payment before? Do you think there was any doubt in his mind as to the authenticity of the cable?'

'No,' he said. 'He assured me that the transfer itself was perfectly in order. And he actually told me – I remember now you've explained it – that the reason for the delay was simply an internal matter between his bank and the Hang Seng, and he was really apologetic, saying he couldn't pay out when he didn't know whether or not the Hang Seng had sufficient money with them to cover.'

'Well, that's it, then. The cause of your worry is that you don't understand the mechanisms involved. I'll tell you something else. If the codes had been wrong – but remember that we knew one hundred per cent that they were not – he would have telephoned the Hang Seng as soon as the cable came in and he could have done so before the bank in Hong Kong had closed. If it had been closed, he could have telephoned the bank manager at home. If they had been wrong, you wouldn't be here now. Unless, of course, he decided to play it cool and you were followed. Were you followed?'

'No. I checked. I definitely wasn't.'

'When you go back to the bank now, you won't be arrested. If what you have told me is correct, there is no possibility of that whatsoever.'

'What about tomorrow?'

'If he thought anything was wrong, he would have asked you to come back tomorrow. Anyway, I'm giving you the facts as I see them. Whether or not you want to go on with the job is up to you. But I do strongly suggest that you go back to the bank now, then to the diamond merchant. If, having seen the manager, you don't like your impressions, I've got a car here. You can collect your things and return with us.'

He did not ask from which direction I had come. Possibly he imagined that I was based in Amsterdam.

'In any case I'll meet you back here at three-thirty.'

'Do you want me to draw out anything when I'm at the bank?'

'You've just told me he wouldn't pay out.'

'Yes, I know, but he told me I could draw up to five thousand dollars against the cable if I needed it.'

'Which,' I said, 'rather supports his explanation of the delay. No leave it in. You're not in any hurry to get hold of bread.'

'What happens if I do get caught?' he asked.

'You can't,' I said. 'There's no possibility of that.'

'Well, if I did, how would I explain myself?'

'Well, you won't be able to prove that you're an innocent victim exactly.'

We went through several possible explanations in search of one which would demonstrate that he wasn't knowingly involved in any conspiracy or attempt to defraud, but they could be countered by the fact of his false 'Mr John Nicholas Robinson' passport.

'Who do I say I received my instructions from?'

'Anybody. Use your imagination. Okay, describe a man who fits the description of Rod Steiger. Invent any name you like. Say you met him in a London pub.'

I gave him a context, but didn't issue a warning of what would happen if he betrayed any one. From the very beginning Paul had been spared all the subtle psychological briefings. I looked on him as a friend and he knew this. He also knew that if anything ever happened to him he would be well looked after and he had enough common sense to realise that it would be in his own long-term vested interest to keep his mouth shut.

I gave him further assurances – patting him on the back and generating as much calm and confidence as I could, there being no difficulty in this, as this was exactly what I felt – then returned to Hamish. Perhaps, I thought, the situation had been repeated in Zurich. We finished our lunch and I told Hamish that I would be busy all afternoon with gold brokers, so would he amuse himself and be back at the Pop Bar at four o'clock.

At our second meeting Paul looked considerably more relaxed. He was now convinced that the manager had not the slightest sniff of suspicion. Rather, he said, he had been exceedingly apologetic. He had decided that there was no reason why he should not be back to collect on the Monday and made a particular effort to show me that he was now fully restored in spirit, that I had every reason for relying on him and not the slightest reason for worrying.

'I'll cancel the second transfer coming through,' I said.

We returned to Brussels taking the route via Rotterdam, over massive steel bridges and canals, past old windmills, ships in docks, cranes, power stations, poplars, fields dyked and cultivated, and along the flat.

We dropped Peter at the Atlanta.

'Stay in your room,' I told him. 'Have dinner there.

We may need you later. I'll call you in a couple of hours.'

Hamish and I split to our opposite rooms, agreeing to meet in an hour for dinner.

A note on my bed informed me that I had had two telephone calls. They could only have been from Robert Wyndham in London. He would now, I guessed, be worried at not being told when and where to send the two carriers and whether or not to notify the others that were on stand-by. However, Geneva had to be called first for news of Adam. But before this there was something else. I needed a bottle of whisky.

'Hotel des Alpes,' came the voice across the line.

'Studio Two, please,' I said. There was a short delay for ceremonies before I was put through to Tania. The management justifiably prided itself on its friendly service.

'Hello, sweetie, it's me,' she said, with waves of warmth and joy which informed me there had been no tragedies.

'Just got back,' I said.

'How are things?'

'Fine.'

This was a bit non-committal. The truth would filter through leisurely. I was in no hurry. And perhaps Phillip was there.

'How's Phillip?'

'Fine. Do you want to speak to him?'

He was there.

'Well, tell him, yes I do. Tell him that I'll put a call through to him upstairs in a few minutes.'

I heard her relay the message, adding with a huge sense of diplomacy the word 'privately'.

'Had a very busy day,' I said. 'Went out to see some prehistoric caves on the German-Dutch border. Was quite interesting, but didn't come back with the 'photographs' I wanted. Disappointing really, but nothing unexpected. Oh, by the way, did you get your 'parcel'?'

'Yes.'

'Good. Did you like it?'

'Yes, it was fantastic.'

'Are you wearing it?'

'No. I packed it up again for the journey. It's unbelievable.'

'How's your neurotic friend?'

'Thrilled with himself. Absolutely.'

'Bet he is. When are you going to see him?' – meaning 'Can you get in touch with him straight away?'

'Actually, I was going out to have coffee with him when you rang.'

She was about to do nothing of the sort, but the message was understood.

'Oh good. Well, get him to ring me. Yes?'

For the first time, I gave Tania my number. Her briefings had sunk into her so well, that I knew I could rely on her never to use it except in emergency.

'Well, what are his plans? Do you know?'

'Oh yes. I have a message for you. It reads as follows: 'GOOD WEATHER FOR THE MATCH. 150 ALL OUT FIRST INNINGS. UNDECIDED ABOUT SECOND INNINGS AS THEIR DEMON BOWLER WAS OUT OF ACTION. HAVING EATEN TOO MUCH. IS THE SECOND TIME AT ALL POSSIBLE? IS IT ALSO POSSIBLE TO INCREASE IT TO DOUBLE?" '

'Unbelievable!' I said. 'And such enthusiasm! Well, it was straightforward, wasn't it?'

'Completely. He couldn't believe it. Now he's praising you like mad.'

'Of course he is. And I expect he's feeling like a damned fool for all the hell he's created. Well, he's in for a very hard time from now on.'

'You're not going to be mean to him?'

'As mean as hell.'

'When are you coming down? When am I going to see you?'

'Monday; I'll call you about that later,' I said, not wishing the management to know that there was going to be a sudden exodus or anyone other than Paul to know that I would then be in Amsterdam. How's Phillip?'

'Getting very impatient and asking a lot of questions lately. Grumbling about having nothing to do.'

'Oh dear! Well he's going to be up to his eyeballs from now on. How's he going to feel about a repetition of our last marathon journey?'

'I don't think he'll be amused.'

'Anyway, I'll be calling you frequently from now on, so I'll give you all the news later.

'I'm going to see you soon, yes? Promise?'

'Monday, I promise. What are you doing for dinner? Going out?'

'No. I don't feel well. I'm going to have sandwiches sent up,' she said, confirming that she would be going nowhere until she had delivered her parcel.

'Do you love me?' she asked.

'Like hell!' I thought. 'When you've got my hundred-and-fifty grand!'

'Just a little bit?'

'Maybe it will grow when I see the excellent work you have done.'

Kisses came across the line like sheets being torn up.

Adam called.

'A routine job well done!' I said. 'And nobody is more surprised than yourself, eh? God, the trouble you've caused over absolutely nothing. Anyway, just to contradict myself, quite magnificent!'

'I was lucky.'

'Third party?' – in other words, had he been paid by cashier's cheque which he had to take to another bank for cash?

'Yes.'

'What do you mean, lucky?'

'Well, the manager was out to lunch. There were just three birds there. God knows what he'll think when he returns.'

'Haven't you become a bit over-ambitious, wanting to go for three hundred grand on the second shot?' I asked, but didn't wait for an answer. 'Anyway, a repeat is out, in my opinion. Are you agreed?'

Since writing the note he had changed his mind. It seemed to me very unlikely that he would survive the strain of waiting over the week-end and I no longer wished to have to cope with the smallest problem coming from him, as I would have neither the time nor the energy.

'Phillip will drive you back to Zurich immediately. When you've collected your things, re-book for the Monday evening. Say that you will be driving to Milan for the week-end and taking "your Jaguar". I suggest you ask Phillip to drive you to Freiburg in Germany. There's a main-line service from Freiburg, though you'll probably have to change at Frankfurt. Come up here, room 609, Hilton, Brussels. Phillip, by the way, is a bit pissed-off with waiting, so give him some nice chat. Very important. When he has dropped you at Freiburg you are to tell him to return to Geneva immediately. You understand? Say that I'll need to be in touch with him at the earliest. We want no hotel registrations.'

I called Phillip: 'Everything okay?'

'Yes,' he said, without much enthusiasm. 'Well, there's nothing much doing.'

'Good,' I said. 'You've fallen into the trap. You're going to be screaming for peace, sleep and lullabies in the sunshine after the next few weeks. Ready for it?'

'Sure,' he replied eagerly.

'First, you'll get your full instructions regarding purchases and despatches tomorrow evening. I'll send someone down today with all you need. He'll also collect your car. Carriers one and two will be arriving on Sunday evening. Others will follow close on their tail. Robert Wyndham will be in touch with you about arrivals. Before this, in fact now, I want you to pick up Adam at the station and drive him to wherever he requests. Okay?'

'Sure.'

It was eight-thirty. He would be in Zurich just after midnight, Freiburg by two, and back at the Hotel des Alpes by eight in the morning. He would also be wondering what Adam had been doing in Zurich for three weeks, and I couldn't let him suspect that the money for his Monday purchases had come from him; so I decided that Tania should not hand it to him either, but that Hamish, who would be flying direct from Brussels, should do it, making it quite obvious that this capital had been sent down by myself.

I called Robert Wyndham in London: 'What's up?'

'Difficulties in not having precise instructions.'

'Right, they'll be arriving by the hour. You have Adrian Rain and Robin ready? Right. Send Adrian to me in Brussels tomorrow morning and Robin and the next carrier on the list to the President Hotel in Geneva to arrive not later than six, Sunday evening. They are to wait in the lobby indefinitely. Okay? Phillip will identify. You are to establish liaison with him, calling him between four and six tomorrow evening. You'll be sending about two carriers daily. By the way, Adam will be arriving down from Liverpool tomorrow night sometime. I've told him that you'll be in charge and that he is to assist you in any way you want. He'll remain in your room at the hotel when you're escorting the carriers to the station, etcetera. How are you off for cash?'

'Short.'

'I estimate you'll need another four hundred. I'll send Peter over with it in the morning. You'll have to send him on the next plane back.'

I called Peter, booked a call to Hong Kong for ten o'clock, and joined Hamish for dinner.

Chapter 19/'Paint me all over with green stripes'

We had $150,000 chalked up. Not much, but a useful beginning. The second $150,000 was virtually in the bag, and I had no doubts about putting it in for good.

There were just a few small details to be tidied up before we moved off to Hong Kong and consolidated ourselves there. The possibilities thereafter were infinite.

As I dined with Hamish that evening; my immediate aim was to secure his co-operation over the next few days above and beyond his role as chauffeur. My other interest was that he, an experienced businessman and capable organiser should come and work with us. It was coincidental that the latter might be the incentive to ensure the former.

He agreed to meet us in Hong Kong in about a month.

'Would you mind flying to Geneva and picking up Tania and her luggage?' I asked.

'Of course not.'

'Crack of dawn tomorrow morning,' I added, 'and, by the way, could I borrow your car while you're away?'

'Actually there's something else which you could do while you're here, which would be immensely useful. I have to give a considerable sum of money to our buyer there, a man called Phillip. It's not a question of not trusting him. I trust him completely. But it's occurred to me what a disaster it would be if he should meet with an accident, having paid all our bread into his account, which, if anything did happen to him, would remain tied up in his account for years and possibly never be recoverable. The situation is unlikely, but accidents do happen and when we can we should take precautions against them. I would feel a great deal easier if you would open a joint safety deposit box in both your names, so that if anything should possibly happen to him the money could still be withdrawn – so long, that is, as you're around! I'll write you out the necessary authorisation.'

Hamish, willing to be of help in anything, agreed immediately.

We retired to our rooms and I awaited my call to Ben. He was overwhelmed. Our exchange was brief. I told him of the delay in Amsterdam, instructed him to cancel the two transfers on Monday, destroy all incriminating letters, notes, names and addresses in his possession, informed him that all carriers would be arriving at the President Hotel in Kowloon, suggested that he send his assistant 'Mr John Stevenson' out of the colony immediately, and promised to ring later to give exact details of carriers' arrivals.

I called Tania to say that Hamish, whom she knew and liked, would be arriving in Geneva the following morning.

'He'll invite you for dinner. Don't forget it's his birthday, so give him his 'present'. And remember, no chit-chat.'

'I'll be on my best behaviour, I promise. You will take care of yourself? You promise?'

For my own benefit I typed out particulars of Hamish's activities and the instructions I would have to give him at different times. I had made a habit of doing this for each person, the details being many, plans being fluid and my memory being poor:

'Stay at the President Hotel, where I have already booked you a room.

Saturday afternoon:
Ring Tania and invite her out for dinner.

Saturday at six:
Ring Phillip, and ask him to come to you for his instructions on Sunday afternoon.

Saturday at dinner:
Tania will deliver $150,000. Inform her that she will be returning to Brussels with you by car on Monday morning

and that she is to be ready on the dot of ten. Tell her that she mustn't telephone you while you are in Geneva, but tell her she may come around to see you whenever she likes.

Sunday with Phillip:
Show him my letter establishing your authority. Do not give it to him, but destroy it, as instructed by the letter itself. On Friday, Phillip was instructed to draw some cash out of the bank. Ask him to give this cash plus his accounts to Tania, then tell him to be with you at eight o'clock Monday morning, at which time, you tell him, you will give him the funds for his purchases, before going with him to open a joint safe-deposit box.

Monday with Phillip:
Remember to collect the keys of his car.
Give Phillip $150,000.
You accompany Phillip when he makes his purchases.
You take twelve one-kilo bars from Phillip.
You take these kilos bars to another bank and sell them.
[Memo to myself: I have to find some explanation for this.]
The money you receive you bring to me in Brussels.
You collect Phillip's car and Tania and drive back to Brussels.'

Then I typed out his letter of authorisation and those instructions which I had already given him. Those I hadn't I could give him over the telephone when he was there.

On presenting my typescript later that evening I said, 'When you have done what's on the paper, destroy it.'

'No need,' he replied. 'I can memorise it.'

'Good,' I said. 'No need to rush back on the Monday. If you like, break up the journey by stopping overnight.'

On Saturday at seven in the morning Hamish left for the airport to catch his flight to Geneva.

Shortly afterwards Peter left for London with cash for Wyndham.

At nine, Wyndham called to say that the carrier Adrian Rain would be arriving in Brussels at midday.

Half an hour later, Adam telephoned to announce his arrival from Freiburg and to say that he was at the central station.

We arranged to meet on the steps to the main entrance of the Palace of Justice.

I listened to his detailed account of the collection and what he had done afterwards. He had followed every instruction to the letter. Arriving in Geneva he had destroyed his 'John Brown' passport and his internal air ticket from Zurich to Geneva which had been made out in the name of Hans Grohmann. He had burnt both and thrown the ashes into the river. Returning to his hotel in Zurich he had learnt that there had been no incoming calls for him. The Bank of America had paid out without the smallest hesitation, even jokingly.

We discussed Phillip, the assistance he would give Wyndham, his departure for Hong Kong with his bird, his continued anxiety, and, once again, his future. He had agreed, because of the cancellation of his Monday withdrawal, to accept payment for his services in Hong Kong. Before catching his train to Ostend, for London, I took all his Swiss and German small change, dropped it into a sewer, and gave him five hundred pounds on account.

At approximately twelve-thirty, the carrier Adrian Rain rang through to announce his arrival from London. I booked him into the Hilton, where we had lunch. Three hours later Peter arrived from London having made his delivery to Wyndham. I spent the next two hours briefing both, first jointly, then separately.

At eight I rang Hamish in Geneva, knowing that Tania would be with him. She had delivered the money.

'We're both very miserable people with colds,' she said. There was no hidden message in this!

Sunday was a relatively quiet day, undisturbed by any comings or goings. In the afternoon J took a short stroll along the opposite front of the Boulevard de Waterloo and down the Avenue Marie Louise. I made a call to one of our investors in London to arrange a meeting on Thursday. I called Wyndham and instructed him to send the following telegram to Karbi at twelve o'clock on the Monday: 'SIGNING OF CONTRACT POSTPONED UNTIL THURSDAY. IDENTICAL TERMS AND ARRANGEMENTS. ALL IS WELL.' Adam was well. Liaison had been established between Wyndham and Phillip, and two carriers were on their way to Geneva. I gave Hamish my 'requests' for Monday and chatted with Tania at her hotel. I lunched and dined with the two carriers, Adrian Rain and Peter.

On Monday Adrian Rain, Peter and I left Brussels, again at six, for Amsterdam, with Peter acting as chauffeur.

In Geneva, in a few hours, Tania and Hamish, driving Phillip's car would be making their journey up. Phillip would have begun what I had no doubt would prove to be the most frantic day of his life. In Zurich all would be quiet. In London, Robert Wyndham would soon be cursing the fact of an alarm call that I had deviously arranged for him, while Adam would be lying in bed with his bird. In Hong Kong all would be quiet. Ben would not be expecting me to phone for several hours, so would probably be playing golf. Daniel Grant in Korea would be carefully scrutinising all incoming telex messages at the Bank of America, looking for an instruction to pay a hundred dollars to a Korean charitable organisation, signalling that everything was okay. And in Amsterdam, Paul, if he was awake, would be

expecting me at the Pop Bar at ten. This arrangement
had been made the previous Friday. At least I was safe
in the fact that he alone knew that I would be in Holland
on this day and in Amsterdam at this time and place.

Was there any possibility at all that I could be walking
into a trap? I wondered. None, I decided. The possibility
was inconceivable. However, flaws in the theory of the
fraud totally ruled out, and treachery totally ruled out,
I had still taken the normal precautions of not carrying
a scrap of incriminating evidence. Just across the border
we stopped for coffee at a small café, at the back of which
were large dustbins. I set alight to the codes and threw them
in.

We arrived an hour early in Amsterdam. Paul would make
contact on his way to the bank.

We sat in a small arcade adjoining the Pop•Bar and
ordered breakfast. Once again I would be able to see Paul
walking past.

While waiting for breakfast, I left Adrian and Peter, to
make a routine check of any suspicious looking people at
or around the Pop Bar or in the Rembrandtplein. There
were none. I didn't expect there to be. Paul was the only
person who had known where I was going to be at that time
on Monday morning.

I returned to the others, waited half an hour and repeated
the check, then went across to the other side of the square
where there was a kiosk to call Paul. This time, there was
'something in the air' which I didn't like.

'I'm being neurotic,' I thought.

I was on the verge of dialling Paul's number when I
decided that maybe after all I was not being neurotic,
so I idly thumbed through a directory instead. A white-
haired middle-aged gentleman, who looked exceedingly
like a cop, walked past. I got the impression that he had
looked at me with more than casual interest. When he had
passed the phone booth, he stopped, turned around and

waited. I made a call to a friend of mine in the city. He was out. I left. The white-haired gentleman took my place. I went back to Adrian and Peter, exceedingly agitated.

I browsed around in the shadows of the arcade from where I had a good view of the square. I saw two men standing conspicuously on the outside pavement of the gardens in the middle. Should I return to the kiosk? They would be directly in my path. One of them was looking in my direction. I went to a magazine stall at the entrance to the arcade and bought a pen. What the hell was I doing? I asked myself. What the hell did I have to be worried about? Maybe they were cops, I thought. No, not just maybe, but most probably. Even if they were, it didn't matter. They couldn't be interested in me. If something inexplicable had happened, Paul would not have sent them so speedily, so cold-bloodedly, so unnecessarily, to me. Even if he was only thinking of his own interest, he would delay until I was safely elsewhere. My doubts, I thought, were ridiculous. I decided to walk past the two gentlemen.

'Are you looking for a hotel?' one of them asked.

I decided to ignore them. Were they street touts? I wondered for a second. No, they were cops, without doubt.

'Nein,' I replied, turning away, cursing my mistake in committing myself to my lousy German and not to French.

'Hey, Roderic!' one of them yelled as if he had known me a very long time.

Replying or not was of no consequence. The game was up.

Epilogue/A Plot of the C.I.A.?

Paul Cotton was arrested at 1 a.m. on Sunday 4th August 1968. He broke within the first minutes of interrogation, holding little back.

The codes had not been wrong. Paul's performance at the bank had been suspect. The manager had cabled his Head Office in the States asking for a check to be made in Hong Kong. His cable read as follows:

'Today we received the following tested cable from the Hang Seng bank Hong Kong quote
Reimburse yourselves Bank America San Francisco pay us dollars 150.000 a/c John Nicholas Robinson order John Stevenson Habindo unquote immediately after receipt of this cable Mr Robinson called on us and required a substantial amount in cash. Mr Robinson with British passport and staying in a small hotel in Amsterdam opened 3 weeks ago an account with us.
Please check with management Habindo whether this payment order is correct and reply by return cable.'

He alone knew that on Monday 5th August I would be in Holland, and outside the Pop Bar in the Rembrandtplein, Amsterdam at 10.30 a.m.

The fact of my capture, an event which could have been of no possible advantage to Paul, rather a disadvantage to all concerned, including himself, was something for which I had not been prepared. I was prepared for every other possibility but this, and my capture ruled out all possibility of putting into effect what I considered foolproof counter-actions.

I had no incriminating evidence on me; but I had the key to my room at the Brussels Hilton. There the police went and found files, including photographs, of the carriers used in the second phase of the operation. Some had already been despatched from Geneva. At the time of the police discovery three carriers were mid-flight. There was a race against time. Time in this instance was on our side. Fate, however was not. The first of this trio arrived in his hotel room and delivered his goods safely. Literally within a few seconds of successful collection by our agent, the police arrived in the carrier's room and arrested him. He was released on bail the following day and subsequently discharged. The other two of the trio were less fortunate. Their plane had been delayed nine hours in Bangkok. Surprisingly they cleared customs; but they were caught along with their loads two hours later. Two days later they were sentenced, given a choice of six months imprisonment or a fine of $2,500 U.S. each. Ben, still at large, arranged for their fines to be paid. Commendably, all three carriers denied, under repeated interrogation, that they had ever heard of Ben or myself.

The same day that I was arrested Tania and Hamish arrived at the Brussels Hilton after their long drive from Geneva. Tania found a note from me, 'Gone out, back soon'. Thirty-six hours later they were arrested. They were held overnight, then released.

In Geneva, Phillip and two other carriers were arrested. The two carriers were released after two days – they, as others being totally ignorant of the fraud, and gold transactions being legal in Switzerland. Phillip, though entirely innocent, was held for six weeks.

In Amsterdam, the two carriers who had accompanied me there were picked up with my assistance. There was no way they could incriminate themselves, myself, or anyone else, and I had left them without money. They were quickly released.

In Hong Kong a frantic search was on for Ben, with the assistance of every medium of communication. He was caught after ten days and sentenced to four years. The prosecutor had described him as the leader of a monstrous international criminal organisation that spread its evil tentacles throughout every corner of the globe. It was assumed that he and 'Mr Stevenson' were one.

I was more fortunate; I would say, in the circumstances, miraculously fortunate. I received the maximum sentence under Dutch law. This, after remission, amounted to twelve months. During this time I wrote three books, including this one – in a code which later took me over four months to decipher. I am greatly indebted to the several persons I met immediately after my capture and during my internment: particularly to the two members of the Dutch C.I.D., Superintendent G. Toorenaar and Detective Sergeant E. Jagerman, for whose intelligence, sense of humour and decency in the course of their duty in the handling of my case I have high admiration.

In our overall plan, we had failed. The following account, one of several published months afterwards, suggested that we had been doomed even before we began.
It began:
'HOW A U.S. AGENT TRAPPED A BRITISH GOLD SMUGGLER OVER CHAMPAGNE IN HONG KONG.
'The gold bars were finding their way to North Vietnam . . . and helping to finance the Communist war effort, a fact that had not gone unnoticed by the American Central Intelligence Agency.
'The evening was heavy and very warm . . . As Ben Smith and his new business contact sipped their cocktails in the air-conditioned cocktail bar of the colony's luxurious Hilton Hotel, they discussed what was to become of Smith's boldest gamble for the big time . . . A daring plan suggested by the American to crack the secret payout codes of the Bank of America.

'The prospects and lure of the really big kill were too great for Smith to pass by. And in his excitement he did not properly calculate the risks – or even bother to properly screen the identity of his newly-found ally and confidant. If he had he might not have been in prison today. For the man sipping cocktails with him and sharing his expensive brand of American cigarette was a secret service agent of the C.I.A. – on order at any price to crack the British ring whose smuggled gold was getting to the North Vietnamese.

'A DRASTIC TRAP

'The American deliberately gave Smith the identity of the Seoul contact, knowing that he was giving away the secrets of the bank payout codes, but aware that this would be the only way to smash the Smith operation. It would be impossible to pin a heavy jail sentence on the Londoner under the Hong Kong laws for his gold smuggling activities. Smith's cover was too good, and he was at pains never to touch gold himself. In any case, in Hong Kong a person caught carrying gold illegally would be treated under normal Customs and Excise law – and a first offence would not necessarily mean a jail sentence. So the C.I.A. were forced to take drastic and elaborate steps to catch their man. The bank ruse, with untold financial "rewards" for Smith, they calculated, would be irresistible.

'THE LAST CARD IS PLAYED

'Smith followed their plan to the letter, while the C.I.A. agent alerted his superiors that the bait had been swallowed.

'The Bank of America were tipped off.

'In Seoul, Ben Smith made contact with the man who held the secret of the codes and agreed the figure . . .

'From Hong Kong Smith then sent out cables authorising payment . . .

'The ruse had worked. Ben Smith was arrested. He had played his last card, and was duped by a trick call . . . his greed for quick and easy money and a lust for the high life.'

It is very difficult to believe what one reads in the papers these days. But . . . Daniel Grant, the one American involved in the case, was never brought to trial.

*Appendix A/*Technical Documents

[i]

AN EXTRACT FROM 'LONDON OFFICE PROCEDURES', WHICH CON-
CONTAINED MY INSTRUCTIONS TO THE LONDON STATION MANAGER
ON: 'THE DESPATCH OF CARRIERS – MORNING OF DEPARTURE'.

1 Arrangements must be made to meet 'C' at a suitable location not later than 8 a.m.

2 All of the following items must be taken to the meeting: tie-on labels; two packets of dextrasol; needle and cotton, shirt and trouser buttons; belt; shoe laces; – these items to be kept in personal luggage on flight; copy of 'Carrier's Procedures'; suit and corset of right size; four shoulder pads – not to be concealed but packed at the bottom of the suitcase; return boat-train ticket; carrier's cash allowance; one large brown envelope.

3 On meeting 'C', check to see that his passport and medical card are up to date. Does he have required visa stamp?

4 Check 'C's' luggage, clothing and personal effects. Take all diaries, address books, notebooks and cash from him. You will place these items, in his presence, in the brown envelope and seal it. Get 'C' to sign over the seal.

5 Having checked all luggage, you will re-pack 'C's' things.

6 'C' will put on his suit and corset.
   Check the following:
   a That the thigh laces have at least 3 inches of slack when tied.
   b That his vest, if worn, is worn over the suit.
   c That the shoulder straps are not visible through his shirt. If they are, a replacement shirt must be purchased.
   d That shirt and trouser buttons are secure.
   e That zip and crutch of trousers are secure. If unsuitable, trousers are to be replaced.
   f That belt or braces are worn.
   g That 'C' is not wearing new shoes. If he is, then the soles must be cut.
   h That his trouser pockets are empty.

7 Make 'C' walk round the room so that you can get a general impression of his appearance. Instruct him how to sit down and get up, etc.

8 Give 'C' a copy of 'Carrier's Procedures' to re-read. Ask him if he has any questions or worries about anything. You must of course know the answers to any questions on the procedures. You will not depart from these, nor answer any questions on matters which do not directly concern him.

9 Inform 'C' of his destination in Europe, when he is at the station. Do not inform him of his ultimate destination. At the same time, give him his ticket, plus £10 in cash – an advance on his fee, which is to be signed for. Remember that after 'C' has been told his destination he is not allowed to make any telephone calls or to leave your presence at any time (e.g. go to the Gents with him, if necessary).

10 You must arrive at the station at least 45 minutes before the train is due to depart. Instruct 'C' to tell British Authorities, if asked, that he is going to Brussels for a few days.

11 Remind 'C' to get plenty of reading material for the journey; when he has done this, escort him to the train and remain with him at the window until the train departs.

[ii]

CARRIER'S DEPARTURE SHEET, TO BE PROCESSED BY LONDON STATION MANAGER.

'C's' No: ....
Load No: ....
Route No: ....

(i)	Date 'C's' identity card sent to FE	....
(ii)	Date FE notified of L no	....
(iii)	Date EUR notified of L no	....
(iv)	Date of 'C's' departure from London	....
(v)	Date 'C' notified of his departure	....
(vi)	Date air ticket purchased	....
(vii)	Expiry date of 'C's' passport	....
(viii)	Expiry date – smallpox	....
(ix)	Expiry date – cholera	....
(x)	Place of stay in London	....
(xi)	Date London hotel booking made	....
(xii)	Hotel destination EUR	....
(xiii)	Date reservation made	....
(xiv)	Notification of 'C' (3 days before)......	
	(2 days before)......	
	(1 day before)	

(xv)   Size of suit ......
(xvi)   Size of corset......
(xvii) Kit prepared......

These departure sheets were kept at London Office and processed by Adam, who was in effect the manager.

[iii]

EXTRACTS FROM THE CARRIERS PROCEDURES MANUAL, INCLUDING
THE BONUS INCENTIVE SCHEME FOR CARRIERS.

1 AT INITIAL MEETING
Completion of form, examination of passport and dress rehearsal with short practice manoeuvres.

2 FOLLOWING INTERVIEW
(i)   Obtain cholera and smallpox innoculations and produce medical card for viewing by us. Injections in arm.
(ii)   Obtain visas if required.
(iii)   Obtain three identical passport photographs and forward to us.

3 INSTRUCTIONS ON DRESS
(i)   Definitely not to be worn: Vests or new shoes.
(ii)   Always dress 'English', with collar and tie. Avoid casual gear.
(iii)   SUIT. No light colours to be worn. Dark grey or check is advised. Trousers must be smart, *but not tight*.

4 NOTIFICATION OF DEPARTURE
You will be given minimum of ten days prior notice.

5 ESSENTIAL TRAVELLING GEAR AND DOCUMENTS
All of which will be checked before your departure.
(i)   Large case.
(ii)   Small overnight case containing toilet requisites.
(iii)   Coat.
(iv)   Business material depending on cover.
(v)   Plenty of reading material.

6 DOCUMENTS TO BE KEPT ALWAYS ON PERSON
A check will be made to ensure that you are in possession of the following on the morning of departure:

    (i)   Passport.
    (ii)   Visas.
    (iii)   Health card, showing smallpox and cholera innoculations.
    (iv)   Cash between £10 and £15.
    (v)   Boat and train tickets to Europe.
    (vi)   Instructions on how contact will be made, on your arrival in Europe.

7 MORNING OF DEPARTURE TO EUROPE
    (i)   'Suit' must be worn.
    (ii)   You will be escorted to the boat train.
    (iii)   You will not be told your destination until the station, when also you will be instructed on how contact is to be made.
    (iv)   You will not be permitted to make 'goodbye' or other telephone calls.
    (v)   On exit from U.K., at Customs or Passport Control, if asked, you will answer that you are going away for a couple of days (to Europe) and, if you need further qualification of your answer, that you will be staying with friends.

8 ON ARRIVAL IN EUROPE
    (i)   Contact will be made with you, you will be taken to your hotel for the night, or flat, and later for dinner.
    (ii)   You will have your documents and luggage re-checked, and be re-briefed.

9 MORNING OF DEPARTURE FROM EUROPE
    (i)   Two hours before your departure, you will be loaded.
    (ii)   You will be escorted to the airport.
    (iii)   You will be told your destination, and given instruction on how contact will be made, at the airport.
    (iv)   Our representative will check that your luggage is correctly ticketed to your destination.
    (v)   You will be accompanied to last European Transit Port.

10 INSTRUCTIONS ON PLANE AND IN TRANSIT PORTS
    (i)   You are advised not to drink alcohol, and to abstain from eating during the last ¾ hour before landing.
    (ii)   Always move with the crowd.

(iii) When going to sleep – ALWAYS do so with head towards the aisle and never with legs out.

(iv) Always choose a rear window seat, when possible. Cautionary note: on certain trans-continental flights before boarding the plane passengers will be given their own seat numbers. You are advised to seat yourself as instructed and not to seek alternative arrangements. If, following such procedure, you find yourself seated between two other passengers you will need to be more careful about your sleeping position.

(v) On entering and leaving the plane: To ward off passengers threatening to bump against you, hold overnight case in one hand in front of you and your coat behind, or vice-versa and walk or edge your way sideways. On disembarking, use handrails to avoid slipping.

(vi) On board, passengers will find or be provided with *disembarkation cards*. These MUST be filled in BEFORE landing – to avoid unnecessary waiting on arrival. Where it asks 'origin of journey' put London. Where it requests 'nature or purpose of visit', write 'IN TRANSIT TO . . .' unless we have arranged a particular cover for you in which case you write 'Business'. Similarly, Customs Declaration Forms, if provided, must be completed before landing.

(vii) PRIOR TO LANDING: You are advised to wash and shave to give yourself as smart and as affluent an appearance as possible, bearing in mind that in excess of 20 hours will have been spent on flight. Electric razors are always available on board; if not available in toilet they may be requested from the stewardess.

(viii) ON LEAVING PLANE: always carry credentials, including disembarkation card and customs form (if any) in pocket or hand.

(ix) IN TRANSIT PORTS: when disembarking at airports in transit, passengers are provided with BOARDING CARDS. These must be kept safely until returning on board the plane.

(x) IN TRANSIT PORT – INDIA: the plane is immediately boarded by a Sikh policeman, very severe looking, BUT whose sole duty is to prevent plane cleaners pilfering the luggage.

11 LANDING FORMALITIES
On arrival at destination, you pass through the following:
(i)   HEALTH DEPARTMENT: a few seconds. Have
       medical card ready.
(ii)   IMMIGRATION DEPARTMENT: (Passport Con-
       trol). A few seconds. You have passport and dis-
       embarkation card ready.
(iii) CUSTOMS HALL: luggage arrives in the hall. You
       hand your luggage ticket, often affixed to your plane
       ticket, to a porter who collects it.
       The Customs Officer always asks the following questions:
       (a) 'Have you anything to declare?'
       (b) 'Have you any narcotics, gold or firearms in your
       possession?'
THIS IS NORMAL PROCEDURE.

12 NOTES ON THE ABOVE:
(i) *Remember* that the percentages are 99.999% with you.
Nobody ever gets 'stopped' unless they draw attention to
themselves. Where you are going, huge numbers of passengers
arrive every day by air and are treated with great respect.
'YOU' are 'SIR' to officials. Be polite and relaxed with them,
but NOT humble, neither arrogant. *You* are a *Guest* in the
country and are treated as such.
(ii) It is very natural for a new man to be nervous of his
task. The awareness of the weight and its slight awkwardness
make him tend to think that he appears awkward to other
people, which of course is PURELY SELF-CONSCIOUS-
NESS. Properly dressed, there is ABSOLUTELY NO
PHYSICAL DIFFERENCE AT ALL. You may relax with
the fact that your harness has been designed, made and tested
to withstand the strain of five to six times your load.
(iii) The ONLY illegal part of the entire operations with
which you are directly or indirectly associated consists of
entering the country of destination with the intent to evade
payment of duty on the importation of goods. The maximum
penalties in countries in which we operate, or will be operating,
are as follows:
a three months prison sentence OR 18 months and a fine,
BOTH SUSPENDED for three years, during which time no
re-entry is allowed, but after which the case is closed down.
You will be informed of any known changes in penalties. No
offence is being committed in Europe.

(iv) DO NOT RECOGNISE PERSON OR PERSONS
AT AIRPORT.

(v) NEVER IN ANY CIRCUMSTANCES LEAVE
GOODS UNATTENDED.

*   *   *

Payments and Expenses for Carriers
The following statement was attached:
Your basic fee will be £200 a trip. Payment will be made as
follows:
You will receive £10 advance on leaving London and be paid
the balance of £190 either immediately upon your arrival, in
readily convertible currency, or on your return to Europe in
European currency, or by direct transfer to your account in
England, or elsewhere, as you choose.
Within the first four weeks of the opening of a new route,
payment will be made as follows:
£10 advance on leaving London, £150 on the morning after
your arrival and the balance of £40 at the end of the first four
week period from our office in London.
You are paid or re-imbursed for the following expenses:
(i)   Tourist return boat train ticket to Europe.
(ii)   Tourist return air fare to final destination.
(iii)   Up to two nights hotel bill in Europe, per trip.
(iv)   Up to two nights first class luxury hotel at your final
destination.
(v)   Three identical passport photographs.
You will not be reimbursed for any additional travel expenses
or expenses in connection with clothing, passport or medical card.
Remember that in the event of a delay in the departure of a
plane at a transit stop, all expenses of meals and accommodation
are paid for by the airline company.

*   *   *

Bonus Incentive Scheme
The following appeared on the final page of the same document:
We have a gentleman working with us who has previously done
34 trips within the space of one year, working without 'cover'. So
this should give you some idea of what is possible and that
there can be a very remunerative source of income for you

depending on the extent and seriousness with which you participate.

You must appreciate that it is definitely not in our interest to expose you, or allow you to expose yourself, to other than the barest minimum of risk. An average of one trip a month into the same place is well within the bounds of safety for any individual travelling without the protection of a special cover. The frequency of trips you may undertake depends in addition to you your own inclinations, on the 'cover' we can eventually arrange for you.

It is in our interest to keep the standard of 'Cs' high and to retain, when desirable and possible the services of those that have previously worked with us. It is therefore in our interest that those working with us should enjoy working with us and at the same time always have further material incentive for doing so.

We have provided, in addition to the standard basic fee of £200 a trip the following bonus incentive scheme:

(i)   For his seventh trip, each 'C' will be paid an additional £50 bonus for that trip, and similarly for each succeeding trip.

(ii)   At his eleventh trip, each 'C' will be able to invest £235 in the purchase of an additional kilo bar (the remaining 50% of which will be paid by us) and retain £50 of the profit of the sale, and similarly for each succeeding trip.

(iii)   For his twelfth trip, each 'C' will be paid a bonus of £100 in addition to his £50 bonus, and similarly at the end of each successive trip after this.

All of which means that within a reasonable period a 'C' can be earning regularly between £300 and £400 a trip.

'C's' earnings for individual trips work out therefore as follows:

(1)	200	(7)	250	(13)	300	(19)	300
(2)	200	(8)	250	(14)	300	(20)	400
(3)	200	(9)	250	(15)	300	(21)	300
(4)	200	(10)	250	(16)	400	(22)	300
(5)	200	(11)	300	(17)	300	(23)	300
(6)	200	(12)	400	(18)	300	(24)	400

1,200		1,700		1,900		2,000

Running totals:

1,200		2,900*		4,800		6,800

[iv]

THE SMUGGLER'S SUIT: ITS DESIGN AND MAKING. SEE PHOTOGRAPH
OF SUIT AND INSTRUCTIONS FOR SUIT MANUFACTURE ON ENDPAPERS.

The quilting was cut out in rectangles measuring 36 in. ×
18 in. This was sufficient to go round Adam's waist, with a
couple of inches to spare to allow for the shrinkage caused by
excessive sewing. An equivalent amount of rayon was cut out and
sewn to one side as reinforcement. Curtain tape was sewn to the
two edges of the body of the suit that met in the middle. These
were punched with steel eyes, so that lengthy shoelaces could be
pulled through them.

The next step, the most tedious, was to sew the thick tough
shoulder straps on both left and right sides of front and back.
These were an inch longer than measured, to allow for the
insertion of foam rubber padding on the shoulders. The straps
were attached securely by forty to fifty lines of sewn nylon. The
inside of the suits were lined with soft satin. The suits had either
24 or 36 pockets.

[v]

AN ABBREVIATED EXTRACT FROM 'ROUTE PARTNERSHIP AGREEMENT
FOR STATION-MANAGERS', WHICH DEALS WITH REMUNERATION AND
SHOWS THE COSTS AND PROFITS OF RUNNING THREE CARRIERS A
WEEK INTO HONG KONG.

1 You will not be specifically remunerated for your services other
  than in your capacity as a partner with an $8\frac{1}{3}\%$ interest in the
  net profit on the route on which you are engaged.
2 Drawings in advance of distribution of profits: At the end of 2
  months, £300 may be drawn, and thereafter monthly.
3 Payment of balance of full share of profit will be made within
  one month after the expiration of 12 months. Such payment
  will be made in full *less* 75% of what is due on the last 2 months
  of this period. This final balance will be paid at the end of 3
  months after a 12 month period, provided yearly agreement
  has been completed. There may be a distribution at the end of
  6 months.
4 The net profit on which your percentage will be based may be
  taken as the gross trading profit less deductions for fixed
  overheads, running expenses and commissions, estimated on a
  weekly basis as follows:

	£
Your Expense allowance	100
London Expenses	200
Far East Expenses	100
Carriers' fares	1,380
Unspecified Commission (FE)	75
Bank Manager, Far East	12
Telex Charges	30
Carriers' Hotels (FE)	33
Carriers' Fees (balance of)	570
	£2,500

These will be the only major deductions. No commissions re the Far East end, other than the £25 per trip above, will be deducted before your percentage of the net profit is computed.

5 Gross trading profit on your route is severely underestimated at £5,880 a week, that is £294,000 per year of 50 weeks ... thus allowing a net profit of £3,380 per week, which is £169,000 per year, with an 8½% interest worth approximately £14,075 a year.

6 Your agreed advance on account of distribution may be drawn at will at bank used for buying. You will be able to draw, in addition, your weekly expense allowance of £100.

The agreement was designed to be legally binding, though reliance would not be placed on the fact that it was. The signer, as buyer, would not be engaged in any unlawful activity. Its use would be for clarification. It included the following paragraphs:

1 This agreement is for 12 months. No guarantee is given that it will be extended to cover a further 12 months; but it may be understood at this point to be renewable, and, provided that previous agreement has been found to be satisfactory on both sides, you may count on the fact that we will wish to continue, on same, similar or improved basis.

2 Failure to complete 12 months, for whatever reason, whether by 'act of God', as a result of illness, or otherwise, will result in forfeiture of share in profits for uncompleted period, and, if insufficient prior notice is given, will result also in forfeiture of 75% of share of profits due for preceding 3 months. 'Sufficient prior notice', acceptance of which must be acknowledged in writing, to be taken as minimum of 60 days.

3 'Absence without leave' resulting in any delay in despatching

of carrier and therefore reduction in turnover in any week will
be taken as grounds for immediate termination of agreement
and forfeiture of all outstanding monies due. Any unapproved
absence resulting in such loss will be considered as 'absence
without leave'. It must be understood that without absolute
reliability being the keystone of each individual's functioning
in the whole operation no reasonable business of this nature
can be conducted.

4 You will be solely and directly responsible to . . . and will
accept instructions only from . . .

5 You are specifically requested (a) Never to disclose your status
within the organisation, nor to discuss with anybody either
your terms of employment or salary. (b) To refrain from using
your business address for private correspondence or any other
than a purely business purpose. (c) Not to engage in any other
business while you are in our employment. (d) Never to use
your own car for business purposes and particularly not when
you have any contact with carriers. (e) To observe all procedures to the letter.

[vi]

THE NEW GOLD MARKET AND THE CONSEQUENCES OF THE CHANGES
OF MARCH 1968.

When we began our researches and preparations, in theory the
business of gold smuggling was simple.

Gold could be bought easily on the Continent. It was not
allowed to exceed $35.20 an ounce. All the smuggler needed to
know was that black markets existed, in which countries, the
risks attached to running into this place or that, the appropriate
size of the markets, how to break into them, what the price of
gold was – ranging from $40 to $80, in what currency he was
going to get paid and how to get the proceeds of his sale out. In
all matters to do with the commodity of gold itself he could be
grossly ignorant. It was of no concern to him why there was a
black market existing, what the role of gold was in the world's
monetary structure, when South Africa would be disposing of its
reserves of newly-mined gold on the European market, what the
United States balance of payments position was, and so forth.

On a stable scene sudden upheavals started to take place. This
was the background:

For many years the world had been on a gold-and-dollar standard. The foundation of the world's monetary system had been the willingness of the U.S. Treasury to buy and sell gold at $35 an ounce in dealings with the central banks of other countries. The dollar was thus anchored to gold, and other countries could fix and adjust their currencies in relation to it. This was all right so long as the confidence of other countries in the dollar was maintained, while the constitution of the United States remained sound, while she had a powerful economy, and particularly during the time that her stock of gold amounted to two-thirds of the whole world's currency-backing gold.

However, in the ten years from 1958 to 1968, U.S. gold reserves had sunk from 23 billion to 13.1 billion dollars, foreign countries were holding 30 billion in dollar claims which could be turned into gold on demand; reports of internal strife led some to believe that perhaps after all her constitution was not so sound; and her economy appeared to have dangerously weakened.

Countries which had held dollars happily instead of turning them into gold (which costs money to insure and store) with the advantages that they could be invested and serve like gold as part of the nation's reserves (on the strength of which, bank credit was created and paper money issued), were therefore becoming extremely anxious. General de Gaulle, for example, playing a devious game, was cashing in his dollars for 45 tons of gold to the tune of 50 million dollars every month. Speculators descended on the London market, whose dealers handled nearly three-quarters of the non-communist world's newly-mined gold each year, with the same intentions.

There were rumours that the Canadian dollar, the Japanese yen, two of the soundest currencies in the world, and again the pound sterling, would be devalued. The growing conviction was that the world's monetary system was sick ('Not for three decades have the world's financial structures been so shaky', wrote one commentator) and that adjustments would have to be made.

Uncertainty became the nature of things.

Some economists were advocating severe restrictions on the sale of gold, including the proposition that it should not be sold at all to individuals; others its abolition as a monetary measure; and every speculation on the devaluation of the dollar implied a revaluation of the metal. Markets could be closed down, and for some time. Licences for buying could be introduced. Some of these suggestions were very disturbing, particularly to us, before we were even under way.

The devaluation rush in November 1967 had boosted the demand for gold on the London Market from a normal three or four tons a day to the phenomenal peak of one hundred tons in one day.

In March 1968 another rush was now under way.

Concerned not only with the protection of the gold market but with the dollar, the London Gold Pool, consisting of members from seven nations, issued a statement that they would continue meeting the demand at the official price of $35 an ounce. The demand was checked.

On Monday the 11th March, speculators bought an estimated 30 tons of gold, worth 33 million dollars.

On Tuesday the 12th, 40 tons.

On Wednesday the 13th, 40 tons.

On Thursday the 14th, 20 tons.

On Friday the 15th, the Chairman of the U.S. Federal Reserve Board flew from New York to Basel to attend a monthly meeting of Europe's Central Bankers, for the first time in nine months. Speculators, punting on the outcome, bought 100 tons.

The London market was closed.

On Sunday the 17th March, at a meeting of the members of the Gold Pool in Washington, it was decided, with the prime aim of stopping the drain of gold from national reserves, that henceforth their holdings would be available for monetary purposes only. It would continue being used for settlements between central banks, exchanged at the fixed price of $35 an ounce, and not be sold either to private individuals or to other governments that re-sold to the public.

It was found either impossible or inadvisable, or both, to stop the flow of gold, either newly-mined or already in the hands of hoarders – much to the relief of a great many. It was agreed, as one report stated, to give it a chance to find a realistic price level on an open or 'free' market.

The solution became known as the 'two tier' system. On the eve of starting we had found ourselves confronting 'the most important gold crisis of the post-War era'. It had lasted 20 weeks, from November 1967 to the end of March 1968. During this time governments or their central banks had lost irrevocably about 4 billion dollars worth of gold from their reserves to other holders.

Before the solution, the situation had already affected us

because of the series of uncertainties which suggested that there would be no business in smuggling at all. When the two tier system was announced our earlier calculations were thrown out of the window and tenfold as many new ones were worked òut. How it was likely, once operational, to affect us, would depend on how the market behaved.

From Monday the 18th March, I began keeping a detailed record of the behaviour of all markets for which figures were available – the following being revised extracts:
THE FIRST WEEK – 18th–22nd March
Quotations on the Continent:

| *Monday* | Opening quotation | $39–$44 |
| | Price eased to | $38–$43 |

By the end of the afternoon the buying spread had narrowed from $5 to $2 or $3.

Tuesday	Early dealings	$39–$41
	Price fell to	$37–$39
Wednesday	Steady price	$36–$38
Thursday	Opening quotation	$37–$38
	Closing	$37.75–$38.75
Friday	Opening	$38–$39
	Closing	$38–$40

The London market was closed and would remain so until 1st April. Tuesday was Budget Day; also the day on which the decision to end the operations of the Gold Pool was announced. On Wednesday, Holland lifted its ban on the sale of gold which had existed since 1940.

In Hong Kong, on the official market the price reached $45.65 an ounce and fell to $44.00. It dropped to $41.90 by the end of the week. *No profitable* run could have been made.

* * *

Very anxious indeed about the new situation, and with an idea of how to overcome the risk of dealing between two fluctuating markets (while at the mercy of a time difference) which could result in our incurring crippling losses at the beginning, we wrote to Kuon in Hong Kong. After giving several reasons for our delay in commencing operations, the letter continued as follows:

'We now require additional information from your good self as a consequence of the new situation that has arisen in Europe.

You are aware without doubt that the wholesale purchase price is now no longer at a fixed price.

'Our problem is going to be, that whereas we may purchase at a favourable price in relation to Hong Kong on a Monday, the market in Hong Kong by the time we arrive on a Tuesday may have fallen drastically. We could make a substantial loss.

'Though we fully expect the "free" market price to become more or less stable after an initial settling down period, we cannot, rely on this.

'We would like to establish, if possible, the procedure of agreeing upon the sale price in Hong Kong *before* the departure of a "salesman" from Europe, a price which would naturally be subject to delivery within 48 hours. Naturally I do not expect a discussion with you on this point in detail until my arrival, but prior to this some comment from you would be welcome.

'Would you also be good enough to send present prices in HK and TKY as well as the prices over the past week since the change.

'Also, can you tell us whether your people in Japan are able to pay in any other currency beside yen and whether you have any means of telexing from Japan to HK. We wish to avoid, if possible, the physical transportation of proceeds from Japan, though we are prepared to do so.

'May I respectfully impress upon you to be specific in your reply to any new situations likely to evolve at your end regarding price fluctuations in relation to those in Europe, &c.'

* * *

THE SECOND WEEK – 25th–29th March
Throughout the week the buying price ranged between $38 and $40 an ounce.

In Beirut, on the Monday, 'very little business' was reported. In Frankfurt, the same day, gold was bought at $37.70 and sold at $44.00.

In Paris, on Tuesday, the headlines covering the day were 'Gold Price Soaring'. The price had reached 6,410 francs per kilo, $40.51 an ounce.

In Milan, on Wednesday, the price reached $41.80 an ounce. The markets in Zurich and Paris were described as 'hesitant'. There were unconfirmed reports that South Africa had decided to split her sales between the Central Banks and 'free' markets.

At the end of the week the price in Brussels was $38.40. By the end of the week the spread between buying and selling prices had shrunk to 50 cents.

* * *

A reply was received from Kuon, who had again just returned from a business trip to Japan:

'There is always a sizeable marginal difference in relation to European prices, which fact you must have noticed in the past, and even at present the same position stands.

'Of course there will be possibilities of fixing certain conditions prior to salesman's departure but this can only be discussed and arranged between us after your arrival.

'The present rate in Hong Kong is HK$8,450 per kilo.

'You will definitely get better offers in Tokyo but I wouldn't recommend to start this operation at this stage in view of the risk you may involve there. I shall be prepared to proceed with you to Japan to make arrangements if you desire.'

Apart from the price, this news was encouraging. The problem of coping with price fluctuations on two markets could be overcome. The risk referred to in Japan was a portable transistorised gold-detecting machine used at Tokyo airport.

Though market conditions were wholly unsatisfactory, we nevertheless informed Kuon, as well as Ben's other contacts that we would be commencing operations as from the 6th May. I was certain that the market would settle, and that it would do so at around $38 an ounce. Buyers on the Hong Kong black market supplied most of the needs of the black market dealers of all other countries in Asia (excluding those in India supplied from Dubai); therefore, even if the price did not settle at around $38 an ounce but around $40, the black market in Hong Kong, dependent upon gold fed to it illicitly from Europe, would have to adjust itself favourably enough to make it worth while for European operators to continue supplying.

There was still information I needed from Kuon, so, while informing him when to expect us, we wrote the following:

'I must beg the favour of your assistance once again in supplying us with some answers to the following questions which we are unable to obtain on our own here.

'What, briefly, is the relationship between the unofficial and official markets at your end? And therefore the relationship between the unofficial price for the finest 9999 merchandise and the official price for whatever quality merchandise is quoted for example in the *South China Morning Post* and infrequently in the British *Financial Times?*

'Is the unofficial price always higher? And why?

'Without this knowledge we cannot make a proper assessment of the relatedness of the two markets, and we would therefore be much obliged once again for your kind co-operation.'

*　　*　　*

THE THIRD WEEK – 1st–5th April
The London market re-opened, with two price fixings a day instead of one, at 10.30 a.m. and 3 p.m. The prices during the week were fixed as follows:

Monday	10.30	$38.00	At the close, a price of $37.50–
	3.00	$37.70	$37.80 was quoted.
Tuesday	10.30	$37.60	
	3.00	$37.30	$37.50–$37.80
Wednesday	10.30	$37.70	
	3.00	$37.60	$37.00–$37.50
Thursday	10.30	$36.70	
	3.00	$36.95	$36.90–$37.20
Friday	10.30	$37.20	
	3.00	$37.00	$37.00–$37.30

The Zurich market, the most important after London, had moved close in line with its giant rival. The spread between buying and selling prices had shrunk to 30 cents.

On Wednesday, conditions were described as 'quite active' following news from Hanoi of their willingness to meet the Americans.

As a result of this news the price had opened at a dollar lower the next morning.

On Friday, following reports of trouble in the United States and the assassination of Dr Luther King, there had been much speculative buying. The price fell back later in the day.

In Hong Kong, the official price averaged 303.25 HK$ a tael, U.S.$41.10 an ounce. *Business between Europe and Hong Kong could have been done profitably on any load of fifteen kilos upwards* (at $38 an ounce a load of 15 kilos would cost £7,635).

*　　*　　*

The following significant reply arrived from Kuon:
'I am glad to note that you have everything arranged satisfactorily.

'As regards the question of "official" and "unofficial" markets at this end:

'The "unofficial" price is the black market price. The "official" is that set up by the government, which is usually between ¼% and 1% lower than the "unofficial". The latter rate is that at which authorised banks make settlements of export bills and drafts.

'We only have fineness of 9.45% purity on the official market, which is called "Industrial G", and considered legal for transactions. Whereas 9999 being concerned, we usually get a premium on percentage of fineness and this is based on the daily quotations as published in the South China Morning Post.

'Unofficial prices are always higher than official prices as the authorities will make periodical adjustments whenever the difference exceeds 1½%, thus to bring the official price within limits. Therefore the official rates are more or less based on unofficial rate fluctuations.'

The fact that prices on an official market were based on the prices on an illegal one appeared strange.

*   *   *

Though the market had quietened since its storm-harassed opening and the price had settled at a reasonable level, it remained obvious, as had been anticipated on news of changes, that the business of gold smuggling had suddenly assumed some complex aspects. The situation ahead was bound to be precarious.

Conditions for the fourth, fifth and sixth weeks after the setting up of the 'two tier' system and the opening of the 'free' market were not encouraging:

THE FOURTH WEEK – 8th–11th April
In London the price rose frantically from $37.00 to $37.70 over the first half a dozen fixings, but shot up on the Thursday when at the close before the Easter weekend it was quoted at $38.00–$38.30, reaching its highest level since the opening of the London 'free' market. That was probably due to the belief that South Africa would be selling no gold at all for the time being.

The prices on the Zurich and Paris markets kept in line.

Business between Europe and Hong Kong could still have been profitable on any load of 15 kilos upwards.

THE FIFTH WEEK – 16th–19th April
The London price fluctuated between $37.55 and $38.10. The official price in Hong Kong had gone down to $40.10 an ounce

by the end of the week. *Only during the early part of the week could business have been profitably done, even on a maximum load.*

THE SIXTH WEEK – 22nd–26th April

The sixth week was ushered in with the headlines ' "FREE" GOLD WILL GET ITS FIRST REAL TEST.' 'The question mark over this week is whether gold fever will grow enough to push up the price to a level which might tempt South Africa to start selling again. And if so where? (London or Zurich)'. Both the American and British governments were attempting to pressurise her into doing so, hoping to push the price below $35.00 an ounce.

In Zurich on the Monday, the price jumped a dollar.

The average buying price in London during the week was around $38.50. The official price in Hong Kong was just over $41 an ounce. *Only a loss could have been incurred on a run between the two markets.*

It had to be borne in mind that each jump of a dollar per ounce meant an addition of $32 on the cost of buying each kilo and therefore $768 on each full load.

The situation ahead was bound to be difficult.

Appendix B/Autobiographical Note

Search for Truth

I had read in the *Rubaiyat* of Omar Khayyam the following lines:

'Myself when young did eagerly frequent
Doctor and Saint, and heard great Argument
About it and about, but evermore
Came out by the same door as in I went.'

I could not accept the implications of this. There were answers, they could be found, and I would find them, even though it took my whole life. To seek out truth concerning the meaning and ultimate purpose of life, seemed to me to be more important than all else. By persisting I had to come to some end.

I read, exposing my mind to as much knowledge and as many theories, beliefs, systems and movements of thought as possible. Truth could be arrived at systematically through study and logic, I thought. I came, however, to the inevitable dead ends of a purely intellectual approach.

I became interested in Yoga, found a guru and practised self-realisation through meditation. From the far end of a crowded restaurant in lunchtime London an old man with piercing blue eyes and a mass of bleach-white hair – unknown to me – signalled across the room. He had read, as he subsequently explained, my deepest aspirations. Without any introduction or explanation he asked: 'Are you interested in Indian Philosophy?'

'Yes,' I said.

'Then I suggest you read the *Autobiography of a Yogi* by Paramhansa Yogananda; and when you've read it perhaps you'll write to me. Here's my card.'

And thus our relationship began.

Truth, I readily accepted, was beyond thought; it was transcendental and could only be apprehended directly, not by climbing up any ladder of mental concepts. The way was through more consciousness. The ultimate, though inconceivable, was to become God oneself.

But Yoga meant a denial of the world and the abandonment of reason. If indeed there was any ideal intended way then it had to be accessible not only to a few but to the whole of humanity.

From Yoga I passed through several 'ways', the last of which were the teaching and methods of two Russian mystics, Gurdjieff

and Ouspensky. Eventually I came to believe in the very
limited effectiveness of all systems which to improve the will
depended ultimately upon superhuman efforts by the same
will.

Coincidentally at this point I came across a movement and
process called Subud.

Subud was anti-method; it did not teach so it was neither a
system, a religion nor a philosophy. It centred around the
experiencing of some mysterious life energy which achieved
simply through its presence the same purifying and evolutionary
ends which are generally sought through Yoga and similar
systems. In contrast to these it required no effort of will, rather
the cessation of the will's activity in an act of submission. This
energy could not be called at will; it came in an act of grace
through a form of asking. Initiation took place by being in a
receptive condition in the presence of another in whom the
process had already started.

Did such an energy exist? What was its origin? What were its
effects? There was only one way to test the claims of Subud and
this was to become initiated myself.

I was associated with Subud for about three years. There were
undoubtedly some who benefited from their experience, as there
were others who undoubtedly did not. (The actress Eva Bartok
has written a book on how, within a few days of her coming to
Subud, she was completely cured of a malignant cancerous
growth.) What the force was or from whence it came there
seemed no way of determining. It was undoubtedly real. Though
I spent frequent weeks on end in a condition of high ecstasy,
what mattered ultimately was that over a period of time it did
not seem to have left me indisputably improved; nor did I feel,
after long reflection, that I was moving in any significant, even
definite, direction.

The Struggle to Create – the Search for Fulfilment and Work
I had been going in no definite direction careerwise either.

At first, all I had wished to become was a poet. I had been
brought up on the south-west coast of Ireland, in a world of
great physical beauty and almost devoid of people. I had spent
my days in unrestricted freedom, living out my dreams, exploring
everything that was to be explored, daring everything that was
to be dared, enjoying everything that was to be enjoyed, in an
environment abundant with possibilities.

I fell in love, read Keats, Shelley and Kahlil Gibran, and for at least a year wrote a poem a day.

Then all I had wished to be was a mathematician, then a missionary, then a painter.

By the time I left Eton I had several ideas on what I wanted to do – all simultaneously. When I tentatively aired them, which was all I dared do, they were immediately dismissed as impractical – dreamy, even ridiculous.

The world had been free, but it had also been one of severe restrictions. 'Children should be seen but not heard,' and 'They should not speak unless spoken to,' were two of the many dictums that ruled supreme. Expression was something to be feared.

I had had one practical suggestion and this was to go to University. This would have allowed me to continue with the subjects which interested me and left the final decision about my career open. My ambition was to take not one degree but many.

This request was refused. It was refused frequently over succeeding years.

Given the choice between the army and accountancy, I chose the latter.

My reaction to being an articled clerk, life in a city office and the work expected of me, was one of instant antipathy. There was no need for enterprise, no call for initiative, nothing to strike the imagination, no challenge, and – as I had no intention of pursuing a career either in accountancy or commerce – no redeeming interest. The system of apprenticeship was one of exploitation. Life was restricted; dead, dull and monotonous.

The only way out which I envisaged was through writing – not a very practical view, but then there didn't seem to be any practical alternative. T. S. Eliot had written his *Waste Land* while a bank clerk. I began a poem of indeterminable length, while painting and continuing with my private studies. What I did in fact was to take myself through my own equivalent of a university course, the difference being that there was to be no degree at the end of it. I took excessive liberties with my employer's time, disappearing for days on end. Then one day, after four years, I resigned; and in doing so forfeited the small family allowance that had been keeping me alive.

Within a few weeks, with five pounds of my own money and a hundred borrowed, I found premises and opened an art gallery. At the same time, I knew one artist, one dealer, no collectors and no critics.

Two months later I found two partners and together we produced exhibitions once a month along with lavish catalogues. Eighteen months later, I sold out. I had learnt that promoting artists with little capital was a losing proposition.

During my time in the gallery I had begun writing as a critic. I had also become acquainted with an Italian artist living in London. Three years later we set up the Centre for Advanced Creative Studies, the object of which was to conduct and promote research into the use of new materials and techniques in both environmental and purely aesthetic construction. In the meantime I travelled around Europe trying to make a living as a picture dealer as well as continuing to write as an art critic. In 1963, I attended the International Conference of Art Historians, Aestheticians and Critics at Rimini as a guest of the Italian Government.

I was broke. I applied for a job with the Fine Arts Department of the British Council with letters of reference from Sir Herbert Read, the leading art critic, from the head of a division of UNESCO in Paris and from the secretary of a London art society. I was shortlisted to three and then turned down because, as I was belatedly informed, the job required a degree. Thus ended my visions of a career.

I decided to take any job that would make money and enable me to continue with the research and writing on which I had worked for years. This idea was brought rudely to a halt, when one day every word I had ever written, filling two suitcases, was stolen from the boot of a car.

I had to start again from scratch. And for the next two years, while supporting myself through a series of jobs, I began a work on psychology entitled *Research into Creative Processes*.

I then took a training course and went to teach English in Algiers.

Life as a Game – Algiers – Crime as Sport
It was in Algiers that my outlook on life began to change – and new aspects of character to emerge.

The School, part of an international organisation, taught over five hundred adult students. Teaching came naturally. I excelled at it and enjoyed it. I felt the first real freedom with people that I had always felt in the world of ideas and nature. In learning and developing direct-method techniques of language training, I acquired a sudden taste for dramatic performances. Learning to create situations, emphasising and exaggerating expressions was part of the process.

Though I became increasingly identified with the working of the school, my main preoccupation was still continuing with my research. I had also begun an experiment, which lasted three months and meant that during this period I slept no more than two hours a night, so had considerable time for work. Life was still something to be lived seriously. However, I began to see it also as a series of interesting games, and this is what it became, increasingly.

Games went on endlessly, seeming to provide most of the foreign community in Algiers with its raison d'être. I became their chief instigator.

One incident was utterly trivial, but through it and without any motive of material gain I acquired my first introduction to crime as a sport.

There had been three thefts of money from the secretary's desk. Security in the school was wholly inadequate. Everybody agreed on this, except for the director who did not like to have such inadequacies pointed out to him and therefore obstinately refused to take the simple steps necessary to improve them. The accusations that followed the thefts had considerably undermined morale.

'The cash'll be permanently locked in the drawer,' said the director. 'I'll keep one key and the secretary'll keep the other.'

This was no solution. The drawer, I implied could be opened with a feather.

One day the director returned to the school and was informed to his utter disbelief that once again the money had gone.

I was above and beyond suspicion as I had spent the whole morning with the director at his flat and the whole afternoon with him around town. For ten minutes at lunchtime we had visited the school, during which time I had not been out of his sight. In fact I had been sitting at the secretary's desk chatting to the director and another, who were seated around it.

The enquiry that followed was intriguing and I was able to sit back in safe comfort, and watch it.

A week later I was in Vienna, with leave of absence for a month. While there, the following letter arrived from one of the teachers. He seemed to have been left in no doubt.

'As for the stolen money, "the director" suspects neither you nor me and rose to unprecedented heights of stupidity by fixing

Nelly (subsequently arrested and deported as a suspected C.I.A. agent) with his beady eyes and saying "Tell me honestly, Nelly, did you have anything to do with that business?"

'I'm 94% sure you did it actually – disregarding a 3% chance I did it whilst in a coma, 1% James Mash did it and 2% Nelly. I find your 94% amusing, cleverly done and wholely admirable in the very careful thinking out which went into it – and of course the skilful bringing of George to a position of semi-dependence on your old Etonian shoulder.

'Sherlock is dead, but his spirit, if lamentably diluted, lives on in the writer of this letter. A dissertation on the part of this writer to the spring meeting of the Sir Arthur Conan Doyle Society, under the title of "The Extraordinary Events at Boulevard Telemy", will I feel be of considerable interest to all mourners of our deerstalkered idol; and I shall endeavour to give my audience full satisfaction from their purses, without, of course, being so vulgar, or lacking in finesse, as to give tongue to my own admiring suspicions.'

Two months later I returned to Algiers, having spent a month teaching in London.

There was a military coup in which Boumedienne had brilliantly and bloodlessly deposed Ben Bella. A coup fever was in the air, which left few unaffected. The school, which had a new director in my absence, was going rapidly downhill, being thoroughly mismanaged.

'He should be removed,' said some bright spark.

'He should,' I agreed.

'If you do it, we'll back you,' said two bright sparks.

I agreed.

What followed had all the ingredients – except murder – of several excellent farces and Machiavellian dramas all together, which possibly gave those involved the most memorable few months of their lives.

The chairman of the organisation – who had been summoned by myself – finally arrived from London. He had been slow to respond; but informed that his director was to be put forcibly on the next plane out, he had been left with no choice.

'I am indebted to you,' said the chairman, 'for being the only one here who seems to have taken the interests of the school to heart; though I am amazed by the extreme ruthlessness of your methods. Because of this I really cannot allow you to appear to have succeeded.'

I was the villain. The director was reinstated. A month later he resigned for purely personal reasons. Shortly afterwards I left Algeria and the course of my life became somewhat disrupted.

A Crime of Passion – Vienna
I arrived in Rome where, with references from my former chairman, I acquired a similar job teaching. Before taking it up I went to Vienna. Here I became involved in a course of events which nearly cost several years of my life.

For the past eighteen months I had been in love with a young Austrian Baroness. She was poor, lovely, deep-feeling and deep-thinking, and we shared most interests and passions. We met in England. Since then, letters had flown voluminously, calls costing more than air fares had been exchanged and I had made several visits. The affair had shown no signs of dissolving, rather the reverse. Whilst in Algeria I had taken the equivalent of a quantum jump in physics and decided to become a Roman Catholic. I received instruction in the faith from a Benedictine monk. The a priori assumptions essential to the faith, once accepted, become like an unshakeable rock, and everything else fell easily and rationally into place. Being religious herself, and as actively concerned with issues of faith and ultimate religious concepts as I was, our affair had become more than just an affair of the heart or a romantic trip to which we had both given imaginative colour. It had become like a rock, unshakeable and certain, upon the basis of which every aspiration for the future, spiritual and otherwise, rested. Our souls had become merged together in a mystical bond and they would be forever inseparable.

In reality, however, there was no basis at all and it appeared very unlikely that there ever would be, as every conceivable practical object stood in the way. So, if we could neither be nor become as we wished, and there was no hope, because somewhere along the line hope had been lost, then we would die.

On a crowded train from Vienna I plunged a knife into her chest towards her heart, intending to kill her, then myself. Her words were, 'I love you. I love you. It is not the end yet.' I realised she was not going to die. By some miracle the blade had missed her heart. By some other miracle I was unable to repeat the act.

Subsequently informed that charges would not be brought I left for London two days later. Deciding that they had to be brought, I reported and publicised the incident and returned a month later to Austria, leaving no alternative but that I be arrested and prosecuted. This was now a matter for the State.

I wasn't quite sure what lines I should take, but found a game interest in the situation.

'Ten years you will receive,' boomed the Judge of Instruction, unethically and in exasperation across the courtroom. (I don't think he had encountered a similar set of circumstances before.) 'Ten years and all you are doing is sitting there answering questions like some Delphic oracle. Indeed, making matters worse for yourself.'

Perhaps I had nothing to lose, as all had already been lost.

'I'm not interested,' I boomed back, crashing my fist on the table. 'Ten years, twenty years, it's of no consequence.'

Achieving Carte Blanche

Miraculously, after three months, I was back in London, and from there I proceeded to Ireland, where I remained for six months.

I wrote prolifically, pouring forth ideas and emotions, but having lost interest in earlier research which needed years to bring to a conclusion.

I was in several minds.

The situation in Austria was still unresolved.

Practical life was notable for its lack of alternatives. I could find no job with any reasonable prospects in any way related to anything in which I was interested and simply to take any job was no solution. Work had meaning because first of all it provided an outlet for my creative energies and in doing so offered a means of fulfilment. As for anything else I might have done, I was without the resources.

Perhaps I should commit myself irrevocably to some ascetic brotherhood. No, this was not the way and I would kill this 'pursuit of truth' bug by hitting it hard on the head once and for all. Man's search for truth is doomed to come to nothing. The ultimate destiny of all men, like that of the sun, the stars, all systems, all universes, is simply to burn themselves out. There are no ultimate imperatives which oblige man what to be, what to do, how to live. Everything is ultimately permitted and nothing ultimately matters.

I now had carte blanche. If life had no inherent or ultimate meaning, then it could have whatever meaning I chose to give it.

I was not rooted in the world, nor in any way of life. If I could not fit into the world on my own terms, or even on any reasonable terms, then I could exist apart from it and act in spite of it.

Perhaps I should opt right out.

First Fantasy Operation

'Aufmachen Sie!' a voice said abruptly.

The game was up. The voice, that of a customs man at the Austrian border was directed at my companion. I was in the boot of the car, a large Mercedes Benz. If I was going to die, then it was going to be in Austria.

To get there, being out of funds and banned from entry, it had been necessary to mount an operation, something that required the co-operation of others along with their backing, and so I had concocted a fantastic proposition.

I had arrived in London and eventually made contact with the head of a South London gang.

'In a village somewhere on the Continent,' I began, 'there is a small castle. It's really a chateau. I've stayed there several times. I know the family that own it and the house inside out. I know the daughter very well. Once she took me into her mother's room. We happened to be discussing jewellery, whereupon she came to the subject of her own family's heirlooms. The walls are lined with wooden panellings. She pulled back her mother's bed, slid open a section of them and, lo and behold, there was a safe in the wall. She knew the combination because she had watched her mother open it several times, just as I watched her then. Get the picture? Anyway, she pulled out a very impressive collection of necklaces, brooches, diamonds, rubies and emeralds, insured, I discovered, for around ninety thousand pounds. Once in the house, the job would be a complete walkover. Interested?'

Every detail of the story was fictitious. However, my contact was convinced. An operation was mounted, part of which involved getting me across the German and Austrian borders – the first of which we had already passed.

'Aufmachen Sie!' The voice was no less abrupt, and by now more insistent.

'I've lost the key,' said my companion. This was no good. He opened up. There was a tap on my shoulder. We were summoned to the guard house. They had already viewed my companion's passport and now wished to see mine. It was past midnight.

'Where are you going?' I was asked.

'Vienna.'

Next followed what can only be regarded as an extraordinary sequence of events in the circumstances. The customs man, who had been joined by some gendarme, smiled. I was asked no further questions. My small suitcase which might have contained contraband, illicit money or anything else was not examined. 'Enjoy your stay sir,' he said. We returned to the car. I sat in the front seat instead of the boot, and we journeyed on.

Once in Vienna, I changed my mind and decided to leave Austria. Being the key figure in the costly operation that had been mounted, my sudden disappearance left my new associates perplexed, then anxious, and finally frothing at the mouth.

Resolution

I was back in London and had returned to my senses.

I was twenty-seven and penniless. I would solve the basic material problems of survival once and for all, and buy the freedom and resources to do as I wished in life. I would make money and concentrate solely on doing this. I would make a million. No, ten million. How I did it really didn't matter.

I took up gambling, found that I was in luck, and continued from there.